OVER
EUROPE

TEXT BY
JAN MORRIS

FOG CITY PRESS

Published by Fog City Press
814 Montgomery Street
San Francisco, CA 94133 USA

Chief Executive Officer: John Owen
President: Terry Newell
Publisher: Lynn Humphries
Managing Editor: Janine Flew
Art Director: Kylie Mulquin
Editorial Coordinator: Tracey Gibson
Editorial Assistant: Kiren Thandi
Production Manager: Caroline Webber
Production Coordinator: James Blackman
Sales Manager: Emily Jahn
Vice President International Sales: Stuart Laurence
European Sales Director: Vanessa Mori

Project Coordinator: Sarah Anderson
Project Designer: Jacqueline Richards

ISBN 1 876778 69 5

Color reproduction by Bright Arts Graphics (S) Pte Ltd
Printed by LeeFung-Asco Printers
Printed in China

A Weldon Owen Production

Captions

Page 1: These introverted farm buildings, facing each other across large courtyards, are between Leipzig and Dresden in eastern Germany. This kind of farm is called a *Vierseithof*. Its half-timbered buildings are easier to manage set around a quadrangle, but one of the original purposes of the design was for protection against attack.

Pages 2–3: A lighthouse stands like a sentinel on the Ile d'Ouessant, the most westerly corner of France. Surging around it are the waters of the Atlantic as they approach the English Channel. The island is known as Ushant in English and Enez-Heussa (Terror Island) to the Bretons.

Pages 4–5: Looking across Budapest at night we see the illuminated spire of the medieval Gothic St Matthias Church. The church commands a central location overlooking the city atop the ancient Castle Hill (*Várhegy*) on the Buda side of the Danube.

CONTENTS

THE SHAPING OF EUROPE

Europe is an invention, merely a small part of the great landmass that extends from the Atlantic to the China seas, arbitrarily defined and called a continent. Nevertheless from classical times its inhabitants believed themselves, like others elsewhere before and since, to be living at the world's apex; the name Europe, given to the place by the Greeks, is generally supposed to have meant "mainland," implying that everywhere else was, so to speak, offshore.

There is certainly something absolute to the shape of Europe. In the west it dies romantically away, beyond the surf-fringed Atlantic countries, in those western isles so dear to mythologists down the ages—Hebrides and Tenerife, Spitsbergen and volcanic Iceland, spouting fire and smoke halfway to Greenland. In the south it is bounded by the Mediterranean, which it also speckles with its own legendary islands—Crete, Malta, Corsica and a hundred more. In the north it marches away heroically into the wastelands of the Arctic. Only in the east are its limits less explicit, and even there, apart from the protrusion that is Turkey-in-Europe, for the moment the continent may be said to end where Russia begins. When an east wind blows over County Donegal on the Atlantic coast of Ireland, its bitter breath has often come direct across plain, hill and sea from the Ural Mountains on the far side of Moscow.

Europe is the second smallest of the continents— about one-eighth the size of Asia—but many kinds of terrain can be found within it. Much of it is gentle rolling country, watered by easy rivers, blessed with temperate weather and generally free of natural dangers. There are, however, extremes and exceptions too. There are the marshes of the Danube and the lake-forests of Finland. There are the

SHIPKA PASS, Bulgaria

Above Shipka Pass, in the heart of the Balkan mountain range, is a monument to Russian soldiers
and Bulgarian volunteers who died here in the winter of 1877–78 during the Russo-Turkish war.
The pass connects the town of Gabrovo in the north with the Valley of Roses in the south.

tremendous Hungarian plains. There are snow-peaks and tundras and patches of moorland wilderness. Bears, bison, water buffalo, wild cats, wolves, jackals, Arctic foxes, elks, reindeer, chamois, wild pigs, even a few wild camels are all to be found in Europe, and its coastlines range from subtropic Mediterranean havens to the fierce and awful fiords of the frozen north.

Nevertheless, more than any other of the earth's continents, Europe has been shaped by humans. Its civilization has been nurtured in towns and cities, and all along the river valleys of this continent, on estuaries and sheltered bays, wherever the soil was rich, the terrain safe and welcoming, humankind settled in urban patterns. Half the greatest cities on earth, if not in size at least in stature, are to be found in Europe, in some of the most congested of all habitations. It is as though the river of history, restlessly exploring these countrysides, has left its fertilizing silt to generate streets, squares and towers everywhere from Gdańsk to Gibraltar.

It is almost impossible to imagine Europe uninhabited, and in fact an astonishing variety of the human race inhabits it. "Caucasian" has lately replaced "European" as an ethnic

SANS SOUCI PALACE, Potsdam, Germany

Sans Souci Palace in Potsdam, southwest of Berlin, is the pride of old Prussia. The single-story rococo summer palace was built in 1747 by the architect Georg Wenzeslaus von Knobelsdorff to the plans of Frederick the Great. The gardens are ordered around a former terraced vineyard, and the whole complex of building and parklands covers 716 acres (290 hectares). In August 1991, 205 years after his death, Frederick's remains were ceremoniously returned to his home here.

category on immigration forms; and just as well, for there are almost as many European peoples as there are European landscapes, and they constitute about one-tenth of the earth's total population. The original inhabitants of Europe were overwhelmed millennia ago by successive streams of immigrants out of Asia, gradually resolving themselves into the linguistic and racial groups we recognize today— Teutons, Latins, Slavs, Celts, Greeks. These groups evolved still further into Germans or Italians, Serbs or Norwegians, and threw off a myriad ethnic and linguistic splinters, like the slant-eyed Lapps and the enigmatic Basques, whose language remains to this day unintelligible to almost everybody but themselves.

The Europeans have never become homogenized into a distinctive type. There are Europeans variously pale-faced, olive-skinned, congenitally tall, genetically squat— Europeans who look like Arabs or Eskimos. It can be said that some Europeans are habitually reserved, like Englishmen, or famously volatile, like Italians, or emotional, like Poles, or stubborn, like Turks. At least thirty-five languages are spoken on this continent, almost all with their own literatures. Styles of architecture, cuisines, tastes, attitudes, all vary more widely and abruptly in this relatively small slab of country than anywhere else on earth. They drive on the left in Ireland. They eat boiled sheep's offal for breakfast in Scotland. They are constitutionally neutral in Switzerland. There are eight European hereditary monarchies, besides sundry princedoms and dukedoms. Francs, marks, pounds, dinars, drachmas, lire, leva, schillings, pesetas, crowns, florins, zlotys and escudos are all current somewhere in Europe. A couple of dozen separate armies parade this continent, each with its own uniform, its own battle honors and its ineffably martial generals.

The Romans, in the first centuries of the Christian era, did give much of this place a transient cohesion. From Istanbul in the east to Caernarfon in the west they imposed a common system, accustoming their subjects everywhere to the same laws and customs, enabling them for the first time to travel safely here and there, and perhaps bringing into existence for the first time the concept of such an entity as Europe. For a few generations my own forebears, peering painted out of the druidical forests in the general direction of Italy, might just have felt themselves members of some wider commonwealth—if only because it was to Rome, if the need arose, that their more recalcitrant leaders were dragged off in chains.

When the legions withdrew, and Europe fell apart again, this shaky sense of identity was not exactly lost, but was kept in abeyance. The nation-state was born, and for hundreds of years the kingdoms, principalities and republics of Europe fought each other for supremacy or survival, inflamed by dynastic jealousies, or border disputes, or the

PAMPLONA, Spain

Every day during the July Fiesta de San Fermin in Pamplona, in the Basque region of Spain, the *encierro*, or running of the bulls, is followed by a separate event in the bullring. The festival, celebrated by Ernest Hemingway in his novel *The Sun Also Rises* (1926), is now a major annual tourist attraction.

LOOSDRECHTSE PLASSEN, Netherlands (right)

The Dutch are immensely imaginative in their use of water and waterways. They have had to be, for theirs is the most densely populated corner of Europe, and a quarter of their country lies below sea level. This is part of the Loosdrechtse Plassen, an area of seven lakes between Amsterdam and Utrecht, where over the years the dikes have eroded.

PRAGUE, Czech Republic (left)

Prague (*Praha* in Czech) is the cultural center of the Czech Republic. In 1968, during a short period known as the Prague Spring, the city was the focus of European attention. The new president, Ludvík Svoboda, attempted to liberalize Czechoslovakia and loosen ties with the Soviet Union. The reforms were overturned after Czechoslovakia was invaded by troops from the Soviet Union and other Eastern bloc nations in August 1968.

grievance of minorities, or water rights, or simply relative grandeurs. As the American poet Ogden Nash scoffed:
and so it goes for ages and aeons,
between these neighboring Europeans.

A telling memorial to these tragic futilities is the runic inscription carved on the flank of a stone lion in Venice. It records the participation of Scandinavian mercenary soldiers, from one extremity of Europe, at the behest of the Byzantine Emperor of Constantinople from another, in a punitive expedition to Greece. The lion, itself brought to Venice as war booty from Piraeus, looks rather sheepish to be bearing this message of wasted belligerence, and indeed

nothing could be much sillier than the history of Europe between the fall of Rome and the end of the Cold War. Some thirty-six separate sovereignties govern this corner of the world: it is only now—and perhaps only briefly now— that we are once more able to contemplate it as a putative unity, and to view the whole of it from the skies above without being shot down by missiles.

Another poignant illustration of European fatuity is provided by Vienna, the capital of Austria. Indisputably one of the world's supreme cities, haunted by the shades of its celebrated citizens and majestic with official buildings, today Vienna is a political absurdity. A quarter of all

Austrians live within the city limits, and the writ of those mighty offices of state, portentous beneath their emblems of old consequence, in fact runs hardly more than a couple of hundred miles in any direction.

This is a very European phenomenon. It arises in Vienna because this was once the capital of a much wider dominion—nothing less than the great empire of the Habsburgs, which ruled half of Europe. In those days Vienna's talent for pomp, its instinct for hierarchy, the seductive rhythm of its waltzes, the arias of its operas, set the criteria of civilized life for millions of Austrians, Hungarians, Bulgarians, Yugoslavs and Romanians, and to countless citizens it seemed the center of all things. The history that has shriveled it into impotence has had similar effects all over Europe, causing cities, provinces, kingdoms and republics to rise and fall and sometimes rise again, and often throwing whole generations confusingly out of one nationality into another.

The continent is entangled in a web of frontiers. Some of its borders are geographically obvious: the Rhine is one, the English Channel another; the Danube conveniently separates Bulgaria from Romania; the Pyrenees properly

RIVER ARNO, Florence, Italy

The river Arno has flooded many times with devastating results, most recently in 1966. After a flood in 1345 Ponte Vecchio, the old bridge, was rebuilt in its present shape, probably by the painter Taddeo Gaddi. The bridge is a marvelous engineering feat of the Middle Ages.

divide Spain and France; the summit of the Matterhorn is as good a place as anywhere to draw a line between Italy and Switzerland. More often, though, the logic of the frontiers is blurred and anomalies abound. The Channel Islands, close to the coast of France, are British. Rhodes, near the coast of Turkey, is Greek. Gibraltar, which forms the southern tip of Spain, owes its allegiance to the Queen of England, while Llivia, within the French region of Roussillon, is subject to the King of Spain. Some states contain populations speaking several languages—in France alone eight are spoken. Some populations have been repeatedly tossed back and forth between different states. Preposterous corridors have been decreed to link detached possessions of the same sovereignty, and a place like Trieste has been so confused by the exchanges of history that a stranger arriving there uninformed could hardly guess what country he was in. On the map the frontiers of Europe often look like the meandering doodles of statesmen, idling away the hours of a conference, and perhaps that is what they sometimes are.

Yet with frontiers, however artificial, goes patriotism. Patriotism has been at once the glory and the disgrace of Europe, and you feel its ambiguous energy wherever you

HAMINA, Finland

Hamina, a port in southern Finland 27 miles (43 kilometers) from the Russian border, is built around an octagonal open space planned in 1723. At its hub is the town hall (1798), to the right is the Orthodox Church of St Peter and St Paul, and beyond is the white Lutheran church. The majority of Finns are Lutheran; just over 1 percent are Greek Orthodox and about 10 percent have no religious affiliation.

go. It is not an innocuous pride in the beauty of a countryside, the success of an economic system, the glory of a history, the splendor of a literature. More often it is the stirring but irrational devotion to a state—a particular patch of territory, enclosed within man-made limits and taught to think of itself as different from all others. Part of the thrill of Europe is its effulgence of nationalistic display. It is hard not to feel a frisson of Frenchness, for instance, if you should ever stride down the Champs-Elysées in Paris on a public holiday, when the traffic is cleared, the flags are flying, and you can march toward the Arc de Triomphe feeling like de Gaulle himself. But it is an illicit thrill, for more than anything else chauvinist love of country has brought this continent into disrepute, besides slaughtering its peoples by the million and cruelly delaying its fulfilment.

Every degree of state flourishes in Europe, and demands its own allegiance. In and among the great kingdoms and republics are many semi-states hardly less proud of their dignities. Liechtenstein and Monaco, Andorra, San Marino and the Vatican are all states of a kind, with their own stamps and currencies, their own laws and their own ceremonial figureheads—a Prince, a Grand Duke, a pair of state Presidents or a Pope. And far fiercer still can be patriotism among those nations of Europe that are not states at all, but have long been forcibly subsumed into greater political entities. Hardly a week goes by, even today, without the explosion of a bomb among the Basques, an ethnic fracas in the Balkans, the burning of an English-owned cottage by the Welsh or some act of nationalist vendetta in Corsica. These passionate struggles are like after-quakes, as it were, to the terrible seismic convulsions that created modern Europe.

Europe has always been a magnet. It has drawn multitudes of pilgrims to its shrines, and not a few predators to its riches. Apart from the original neolithic inhabitants, its people have come from somewhere else. Even within historic times alien peoples have repeatedly threatened to master it. In the thirteenth century the Mongols, storming out of the Asian heartlands, advanced far into Poland and Hungary and seemed likely for a time to swarm across the entire continent. In the fifteenth century the Muslim Turks seized the Byzantine capital of Constantinople and established an Islamic foothold in western Europe which still survives. And in the eighth century the Arabs and Berbers came via Africa to create, in one corner of Europe, an historical allegory.

The Muslim Moors ruled much of Spain for seven centuries, and would perhaps have ruled France too if they had not been defeated in AD 732, near Poitiers, in one of the crucial battles of European history. By the end of the fifteenth century they were out of Spain, out of Europe altogether, but they left behind tantalizing relics of the synthesis they had achieved during their long presence. It is an ironic truth that of all the cultures of Europe, the forcibly imposed culture of the Moors, blended with the Spanish genius, remains in the historical memory the most suggestively serene—rich in sciences and philosophies, full of poetry and delight, expressing itself in gardens and golden buildings that remain today, absorbed into the harsher beauties of Christian Spain, poignant images of a Golden Age. Perhaps

it never really was one, but still I never travel among these enchanted memorials without imagining what Europe might have been if it had been more relaxed in its relations with the Muslim world.

The rivalries and ambitions of Europe have embroiled the whole world. An obscure assassin kills an Austrian aristocrat in a small town in the Balkans, and within a couple of years men are slaughtering each other in East Africa, in Iraq and in the Indian Ocean. A demagogue comes to power in Germany, and twelve years later the nuclear bomb falls on Japan. The plagues of Europe become the curses of humanity, and in our own time Europe's mass murder of its Jews has come to seem a very paradigm of suffering. This continent has more often had cause to weep than to celebrate, and the lovely landscapes that are spread through the pages of this book are soaked in blood and tears.

Yet the Europeans long thought themselves the arbiters of right and wrong, with licence to command others. In the Middle Ages the Pope had no qualms about dividing the unexplored world between Spain and Portugal. A century

TOWER BRIDGE, London, England, United Kingdom

This famous London landmark, which was completed in 1894, spans the Thames joining Tower Hamlets with Southwark. The twin-towered bridge has two movable spans (like drawbridges) that are now rarely opened due to reduced shipping traffic. This popular tourist attraction complements the Tower of London, seen in the bottom left of the photo.

CHÂTEAU DE CHAMBORD,
Loire, France

Walking along the balustraded promenade
that encircles the Château de Chambord at
just below roof level is like walking down a
street—past doors and bay windows and
beneath dormers, towers, lanterns and
some of its 365 decorated chimneys.

ago Europe thought it perfectly
proper to seize huge slabs of
other continents, declaring their
inhabitants subject to itself, and
exploiting their natural resources
for its own aggrandizement. A
vast aggressive energy emanated
from Europe for a thousand
years and more. At one time or
another European powers ruled
the entire African continent,
the whole of India, the Americas
and Australasia.

In particular the forceful seaboard
powers of western Europe projected
their values and manners across
half the world. The Spaniards
contemptuously swept away the
Inca and Aztec civilizations. The
French established their *lycées* from
Indo-China to the Caribbean. The

Portuguese declared themselves rightful landlords of Brazil. The Dutch commanded an enormous empire in the eastern seas. Even the Danes acquired enclaves in India, and the British sailed out from their islands to rule nearly a quarter of the earth's landmass and govern, uninvited, a quarter of its inhabitants. English, French and Spanish became world languages. European systems of law, education, religion and technology were distributed among baffled indigenes in improbable environments. It became a military commonplace to find soldiers marching in turbans, coolie hats and flowing robes beneath a tricolor or a Union Jack.

Europe, that peninsula of Asia, dominated the world. More important still, it created new worlds of its own. Although the empires retreated as the twentieth century re-ordered matters, the irreversible victory of Europe was this: that throughout North America and in the distant territories of Australasia, sovereign European settlements were there to stay. Great new nations grew up in Europe's image, and the balance of the world was permanently affected. Imagine a United States founded by Asians, say, or an Australia by Africans, and you may realize how fateful have been the results of this particular continent's imperial urges. When in the 1960s the Common Market came into existence in western Europe, people in New Zealand, on the other side of the globe, felt quite disgruntled to be excluded from it.

The personality of Europe is kaleidoscopic, molded by different national origins, rooted in thousands of regional customs and references, embodied in disparate cultures and sealed by the effects of countless wars. Yet there is some abstraction, more than mere geography, which does bind

this extraordinary gallimaufry into a whole. Even Europe's most blazing nationalists would probably admit its existence, and recognize the power of the European identity.

Gibbon defined it as a "system of arts, and laws and manners," but I think it a more metaphysical arrangement. Perhaps it is partly the bond of shared experience. To one degree or another all European peoples share a history. We have by and large fought the same wars, on one side or another. We have endured similar political or ideological processes. Common depressions and catastrophes have oppressed us, and common tyrants have bullied us. The wind makes people in Ireland shiver as they shiver on the Polish plains, and when the Chernobyl reactor blew up it polluted both the vineyards of Bulgaria and the sheep farms of Wales.

But more probably Europe's identity is a matter of theory. The continent is built upon an immense foundation of very old theories, and one in particular used to be synonymous with Europeanness. The spark of Christianity came from the east, of course, but it was Europe that fanned it into flame, and here the Christian faith was formalized, institution-alized, intellectualized and popularized. It is true that even within the faith the Europeans continued to quarrel—the Reformation that split the continent in the sixteenth century reverberates still on Europe's western fringe, where the Catholics and Protestants of Ireland are locked in apparently insoluble conflict. Nevertheless the notion of Christianity has surely been the greatest of all the factors that have distinguished Europe from its neighboring continents. The first pan-European armies were the armies

of the Christian Crusades and, as often as not, the European imperialists sailed out as missionaries of Christ. Europe is the world headquarters of Christianity still, and until recent years it could truly have been called a Christian continent. Only its Jewish communities, the Muslims of its eastern marches, and immigrants from elsewhere would have declared themselves anything else. To a visitor from Mars it might feel like one still. Half the pictures in this book, I would guess, include the tower or steeple of a Christian temple, and often the pattern of a city is built around its presence, just as the pattern of European history has so often been dictated by its passions.

Only in our century have the godless creeds of the Nazis and Communists tried unsuccessfully to forge the continent in other spiritual kilns, and it is still some distillation of the Christian principle that gives these countries a degree of moral cohesion. That the majority of Europeans are now probably atheist, agnostic or pagan has not yet weakened this heritage, or turned its noble monuments into museums. If Europe's cathedrals are no longer declarations of the continent's creed, they still symbolize its identity.

EDINBURGH, Scotland, United Kingdom

The character of Edinburgh (*Duneideann* in Gaelic) is defined by the old town, built during the Middle Ages, and the New Town. These squares and streets of terrace houses in the West End display the harmonious, cohesive design that typifies Georgian town planning.

During the latter half of the twentieth century Europe seemed at times to have lost its dynamism, divided as it was by ideologies, and generally playing a passive rather than active role in the world. It had fallen into what used to be called, in the days of the old empires, spheres of influence; American in the west, Soviet in the east. Japanese and Arab money had also become indispensable. In some parts of the continent millions of immigrants from elsewhere changed the style of life.

Nevertheless, one cannot take a journey across this continent, whether on land or in the air, without sensing the colossal latent power of it. Its 500 million inhabitants have survived all challenges and miseries to remain perhaps the most variously gifted and productive of all the world's peoples. The achievements of its past are stacked up, so to speak, like a reactor, and the energy of all its prodigies seems to irradiate it. Sophocles, Einstein, Tolstoy, Mozart, Palladio, Pasteur, Shakespeare, Michelangelo—the list is like a roster of human achievement itself. To think that one small continent (to parody the Irishman Oliver Goldsmith) could do so much!

Yet to be a European has not always been a source of pride. Americans and Australians have often thought it an effete or decadent condition. Activists of the Third World have thought it distinctly unwholesome. During the past couple of centuries, at least, Europe has given the rest of humankind as much tragedy as blessing, and nobody could boast of the continent's general behavior in our own times— it could perhaps be said that of all man's inhumanities to man, the cruelties of Europe in the 1940s were the worst.

Time heals, though. As the new millennium begins, Europe seems at last half-reconciled to itself. The nations of the west, so long enemies, are slowly coalescing. The nations of the east, so long estranged, are beginning to identify once more as part of the European whole. Perhaps it will all go sour again; the Balkans will relapse into discord; the old enemies across the Rhine will again come to blows; the British will turn their backs on the continent and look to the sea once more. But at least we see in Europe today the hope of a peaceful continental community—a prospect nobody has been able to discern for a couple of thousand years.

This book is a visual record of Europe at this fateful moment. It is the record of an ideal. Only the gods and angels have been able to see it like this before: the whole marvelous place, in all its diversity, surveyed at a divine remove from its squalors and squabbles. It is the nearest one can get to seeing Europe in the abstract, the idea of it rather than the muddied fact; and of course even now it is only the idea of it that enables me, standing on my terrace in Gwynedd beside the Irish Sea, to look east across England, across the Netherlands, across Germany, across Poland, to the marches of Asia where the winds come from, and to feel myself exhilaratingly a member of it all—a European at last.

BERLIN, Germany

Once the symbol of a nation divided, Berlin is now the capital of the reunified Germany. Parts of the Berlin Wall, erected in 1961, still stand as a reminder of the recent past. Much of Berlin was rebuilt following the Second World War, giving the city a very modern feel.

THE LATINS

ITALY ∾ SPAIN ∾ PORTUGAL ∾ FRANCE ∾ MALTA

In the southwest of Europe, between the Adriatic Sea and the Atlantic Ocean, live the peoples commonly called Latins, stereotyped often as hot-blooded, romantic and artistic. In fact they are related more by the common Latin root of their languages than by anything else, and the five countries they inhabit are as ethnically complex as anywhere else on the continent. Greeks, Phoenicians, Celts and Arabs have all settled in these parts at one time or another, adding their own elements to the common stock, and by now a Sicilian, a Portuguese, a Milanese, an Andalusian and a Parisian would hardly recognize each other as fellow-Latins at all.

Geographically, too, the region is many-faced. Its southern shores are, of course, pure Mediterranean. These are the lands of olives, oranges, perfumed shrubs and scraggy goats, tinged by memories of classical Greece. The sea is not always as clear as it used to be, the beaches are often hideously developed, but still over much of these coasts there hangs an almost palpable suggestion of myth. Corsica, the greatest island of the region, is clad with the aromatic *maquis*, the tangle of thyme, oleander, lavender, mint and myrtle that gave its name to the French resistance movement of the Second World War.

Inland from the coasts, however, the numen hardens. Only 40 miles (65 kilometers) from the pleasure-beaches of Spain rise the Sierra Nevada highlands, whose topmost villages

MONT SAINT-MICHEL, Normandy, France

Mont Saint-Michel sits in so many empty miles of sand that it is easy to imagine the speed with which Europe's most powerful tide comes flooding in twice a day to surround it. A Benedictine monastery was founded on the 265-foot (80-meter) granite cone in the tenth century, and it became a place of pilgrimage, a fortress and, in the nineteenth century, a state prison. Thousands of people cross the causeway each day to visit one of France's most popular sites.

are the highest in Europe, and beyond that again stands the bitter and terrific plateau of Castile, full of castles and formidable towns. The coasts of Italy may be benign, but the spine of the country is the severe range of the Apennines, interspersed by a thousand rugged valleys, patched with dark forests and still inhabited, here and there, by wolves. Portugal does not have a Mediterranean coast at all and faces only the stern Atlantic. As for France, which Winston Churchill once called the fairest portion of the earth's surface, it stretches away from the warm Provençal hills above the sea to fetch up on the chill sand-dunes of the English Channel, about as far from the Mediterranean ethos as one could get.

Yet history has made, if not a family of these states, at least an association. In particular it was here, in the swathe of territories that lay in the lee of the Alps, that Christianity, the chief coalescing force of Europe, developed its power and its aesthetic. From the village churches of Malta to the immense and marvelous cathedrals of Spain and France, from lonely mountain shrines to the Vatican itself at the center of it all, the old consequence of this faith proclaims itself here as nowhere else.

ST PETER'S, Vatican City

At the heart of Christendom is this embrace (some say the claw) of the Church of Rome. Built with 284 columns and 88 pilasters and watched over by 96 martyrs and saints, the colonnades of Gianlorenzo Bernini's seventeenth-century Piazza San Pietro reach out from the great basilica of St Peter's, the greatest Renaissance church and centerpiece of the Vatican's 500-acre (200-hectare) sovereign state.

Here too exploded the Renaissance, that surge of all the arts and sciences which was at once to challenge and glorify the Christian creed, and which now makes all Europe a treasure-house of its artifacts. Much of the artistic genius of Europe has come from this corner of it, much of the philosophical and scientific genius too. The navigators of Portugal and Spain opened the rest of the world to European exploration, creating the first of the great maritime empires of history; later the French flag too would fly over colonies across the world; and almost until the last gasp of the imperial age Italy was still collecting territories overseas.

GIBRALTAR

Gibraltar, claimed by Spain (from which it protrudes), is Britain's last outpost in Europe, just 2.5 square miles (6.5 square kilometers) in area. The concrete slope on the east side of the Rock is designed to collect water.

From minute Malta, then, to majestic France, are a congeries of peoples astonishingly inventive and adventurous. Today France, Spain and Italy are three of the chief industrial states of Europe, while Portugal remains agricultural, and the Republic of Malta, whose 385 000 people speak a language derived partly from Italian, partly from Arabic, stands as a reminder that wherever we are on Europe's southern shores, we are never far from Africa. Here two worlds are linked—the warm cherishing south, the hard and thrusting north—and their mingled meanings contribute powerfully to the personality of Europe.

BURGUNDY, France

Tending vines in Burgundy is an occupation that dates back to Roman times. The Dukes of Burgundy used to be called the "Lords of the best wine in Christendom," and their wines were served to popes and princes. Centered on Côte de Nuits and Côte de Beaune, between Dijon and Lyons, the vineyards are not large, and Burgundy's better known labels are among the most expensive in France.

THE MESETA, Spain

These are the last southern acres of the Meseta, the great dry plateau that occupies more than half of Spain. At its center is Madrid, 2100 feet (640 meters) above sea level. South of the capital the red-earth farmlands roll on mile after mile until they reach the wide, sparsely populated Sierra Morena, rising in the distance. This mountain chain stretches 300 miles (500 kilometers) from the Portuguese border to Albacete and cuts off the coastal region of Andalucía from the rest of Spain.

NAPLES, Italy (left)

Above the clamor of its lively streets, the city of Naples takes on an unexpectedly ordered air. The redbrick building in the center is the Nunziatella Military College, and beyond it Castel dell'Ovo guards the harbor.

**THE ALHAMBRA,
Granada, Spain (right)**

A simple geometric roof covers the Palace of Charles V, a late addition to the Alhambra, one of the most exquisite complexes of buildings in Europe. The Al Qal'a al-Hambra (the Red Fort) was the hub of the Moorish kingdom of Granada established in 1238. After the reconquest in 1492 the Spanish monarchs Ferdinand and Isabella lived here for a while, appreciating its beauty. "They lack our faith," wrote the bishop of Córdoba of the vanquished Muslims, "but we their work."

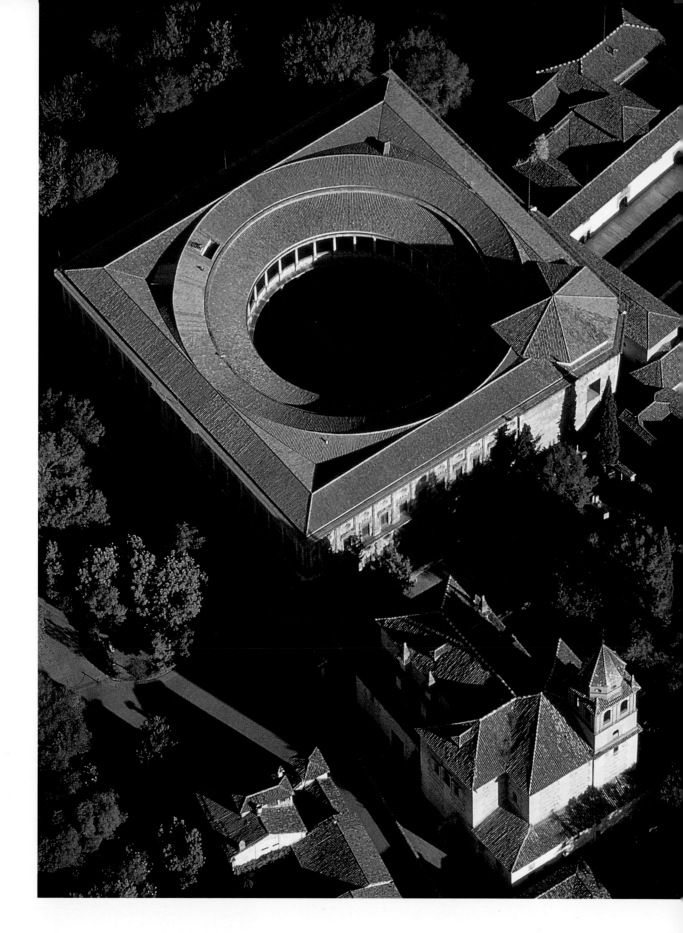

VENICE, Italy

The sun shines on Venice, Queen of the Adriatic, lighting her palaces, piazzas and domes. In the center is the campanile of St Mark's. The Doge's Palace stretches along to the waterfront, where it looks out at the island of San Giorgio Maggiore. The Grand Canal begins at the triangular customs house by the pearl-white church of Santa Maria della Salute.

CHÂTEAU DE LA ROCHEPOT,
Burgundy, France (left)

Flemish-style colored glazed tiles are typical roof decorations in the region of Burgundy, a reminder of the time when the Duchy stretched into the Low Countries. This is the castle at La Rochepot near Nolay just southwest of Beaune, rebuilt in the fifteenth century on an original twelfth-century castle.

GUGGENHEIM MUSEUM,
Bilbao, Spain (right)

This ground-breaking building was designed by the American architect, Frank Gehry, and completed in 1997. The curved walls are covered with sheets of titanium not much thicker than paper. Gehry's architectural sculpture brought new purpose to the old shipping town of Bilbao.

PERUGIA, Italy

The top of a pie smoothed flat by the back
of a fork would look like this church roof
in Perugia. As ageless as the earth, Roman
tiles have given the whole Mediterranean
its architectural flavor. These belong to
Sant' Angelo, one of Europe's earliest
churches, founded in the fifth century as
the glory of the Roman Empire was
crumbling into history. Before then, on this
site in this former Etruscan city, was a
temple to other gods.

MADRID, Spain (left)

Madrid's Las Ventas, a 1929 Mudejar-style building, is one of the country's leading bullfighting arenas. *Corridas* are held from March to October, beginning at 5 pm when some of the heat has gone from the day; cheap seats are in the sun, more expensive ones in the shade. Each event involves three matadors who draw lots in the morning to see which of six bulls they will fight. A resident surgeon and modern infirmary reduce the likelihood of fatalities among the toreadors.

HAUT-KOENIGSBOURG CASTLE, Alsace, France (right)

From its eyrie atop a 2485-foot (757-meter) hill, the castle of Haut-Koenigsbourg has a spectacular view over the plain of Alsace. Built in the twelfth century, it was severely damaged in the Thirty Years War, and it remained a ruin until 1901 when Alsace was, for a time, part of Germany. Kaiser Wilhelm II then had it restored.

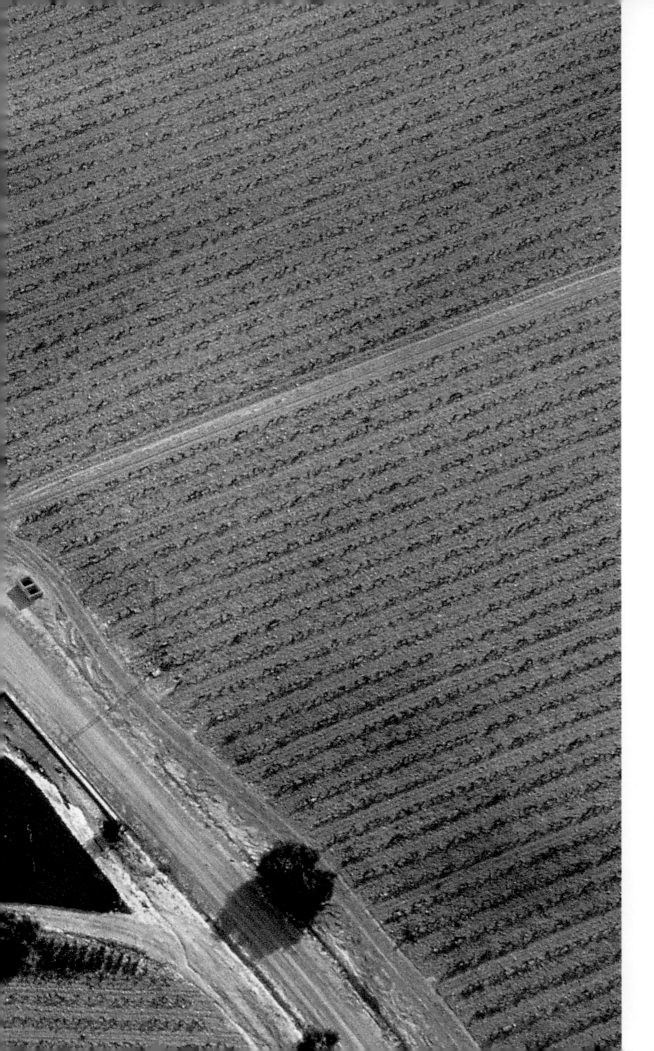

JEREZ DE LA FRONTERA, Spain

An artist could not have chosen a better shade of purple than this to flower against a silvery, parched vineyard near Jerez de la Frontera. Sherry has been made in this southwestern corner of Spain since the Middle Ages, dominated in recent times by dynastic families owning huge tracts of land. Modern business methods are changing their lifestyle, but local pure-bred Carthusian horses remain their passion.

ADRIATIC RIVIERA, Italy (left)

From high above, the serried ranks of
umbrellas look like a strip of needlepoint.
They could be anywhere along the Adriatic
Riviera, northeastern Italy's popular
playground. The 75 miles (120 kilometers)
of lidos and hotel complexes stretch from
the river Po south to Cattolica. The river's
silt accounts for the sandy beaches and has
left the port of Adria, which gave the
Adriatic its name, several miles inland.

MONASTERIO DE SAN LORENZO
DE EL ESCORIAL, Spain (right)

Granite walls, gray-slated roofs,
unexuberant solid symmetry . . . the largest
building in Spain built by the most
powerful ruler of his time is a perfect
monument to the man. In 1563 the austere
King Philip II had the Monasterio de San
Lorenzo de El Escorial built in the
Guadarrama Mountains northwest of
Madrid. Part palace, part monastery, part
mausoleum, it became the burial place for
all but two subsequent monarchs.

MONT LOUIS, The Pyrenees, France

In the decade from 1678, the French
military engineer Sébastien le Prestre de
Vauban set about surrounding the country
with fortresses. This one at Mont Louis, in
the Pyrenees, is the highest garrison town
in France. It served as a frontier post
against Spain, which had ceded its
territories north of the Pyrenees
to France in 1659.

ALENTEJO, Portugal (left)

A lone farm building sits on one of many small hilltops among terraces of orchards, which pattern the landscape of lower Alentejo, southwest Portugal. The healthy soil here has brought settlers since the Romans. But profits from the land are not always attractive, especially when across the Serra de Monchique to the south lies the rich tourist industry of the Algarve.

PISA, Italy (right)

Seen from here, all the buildings in Pisa's Campo dei Miracoli (Field of Miracles) seem slightly askew. In the foreground is the circular baptistery and behind it the beautiful white marble Duomo. This illusion is no doubt caused by the "Leaning Tower," which even now moves one-twentieth of an inch (1.19 millimeters) a year.

PONTEVEDRA, Spain

Every year herds of wild horses are rounded up in the province of Pontevedra, northwest Spain. They are brought down from the Galician mountains to several towns, where they are marked and clipped, and it is always an occasion for celebration. Here, at Bayona-Oya, the "round-up of the beasts" takes place on the second Sunday in June. Hair clipped from the horses' manes is sold to raise funds for the local church. The animals are afterwards returned to the hills to roam free.

ST MALO, France (left)

The nineteenth-century author Gustave Flaubert called this glittering granite outcrop on the north coast of France "a crown of stone above the waves." St Malo is a buccaneering port, built on booty looted from shipping in the English Channel and elsewhere. Once an island, the fortified old town was badly burned at the end of the Second World War. Today, rebuilt, it is a popular resort. The islet just beyond contains the tomb of the local writer Châteaubriand, "Solitary in death as he affected to be in life."

THE LOUVRE, Paris, France (right)

This glass bauble is the solution of the American architect I.M. Pei to problems of access for the Louvre's visitors—about 2.5 million annually. The Pyramid, in the middle of Cour Napoléon, caps a large internal underground area specially excavated and now containing the museum shop, auditorium, restaurant and other facilities. At the same time France's great art museum was reorganized to occupy all of the surrounding nineteenth-century Louvre Palace.

THE ALGARVE, Portugal

Eager to escape the regimentation of their uniformly workday lives, holidaymakers from northern Europe, particularly Britain, have sought their dream villas in the Algarve, Portugal's southern shore. For 90 miles (145 kilometers), along a beautiful and once-impoverished coast, east and west of the town of Faro, there has been more tourist development than in the whole of the rest of the country put together. Here the desire seems to be unanimous: a blue pool, a patio, white walls, an ivory tower and the red roof overhead.

THE DUOMO, Florence, Italy (left)

The Renaissance begins here, at the Duomo in Florence, in spite of a nineteenth-century façade in marble of white, pink and green. Giotto was appointed cathedral supervisor in 1334, and his campanile is on the right. The cupola designed by Filippo Brunelleschi was completed 102 years later.

CONSUEGRA, Spain (right)

The windmills of La Mancha became celebrated when the hero of Miguel de Cervantes' novel *Don Quixote* tilted at them with his lance, mistaking their sails for the flailing arms of a giant. They were a new device then, introduced from the Low Countries in about 1580, some 20 years before the book was published. Hundreds were built, but only a few have survived. In Consuegra there are thirteen. Its castle, which has Roman foundations, belonged to the Order of St John.

ARC DE TRIOMPHE, Paris, France

Seen from here, there is no doubt that the
Arc de Triomphe is the hub of Paris. The
larger of its dozen spokes are Avenue de
la Grande Armée and, on the opposite side,
the Champs Elysées. Napoléon Bonaparte
did not live to see the completion of his
164-foot (50-meter) memorial, with scenes
of his military successes, though his body
was returned to Paris and carried through
the Arc in 1840, four years after it was
finished. France's Tomb to an Unknown
Soldier is here, and a flame of
remembrance is lit each evening.

PLAZA MAYOR, Madrid, Spain (left)

Perhaps it is the unbroken roof line as much as the flat expanse of cobbled square that makes the Plaza Mayor in Madrid look as if it has been superimposed on the city. Building was started not long after Philip II moved the royal court here from Toledo in 1561. Subsequent monarchs occupied apartments above the town bakery, giving them a ringside view of the duelling, jousting, bull baiting and heretic burning that used to enliven the square.

CAMPO DEI FIORI,
Rome, Italy (right)

In the warm morning sunlight, the shouts of the street sellers and the aroma of their produce drift up from Campo dei Fiori in an artisan quarter of Rome: For more than a century a daily market has been held in this "Field of Flowers," brightened by colorful umbrellas and shades. In somber contrast is the bronze statue in its midst. It is of Giordano Bruno, the philosopher, who was burned here in 1600 after a seven-year trial by the Inquisition.

CAMOGLI, Italy

Gray rocks, a gray beach and gray slated
roofs on square housing blocks fail to make
Camogli, on the Riviera di Levante, look
dull. Perhaps it is the splash of color from
the boats and the warmth of the ocher-
colored walls that give this hillside port,
once famous for building merchant ships,
sufficient charm to attract holidaymakers.

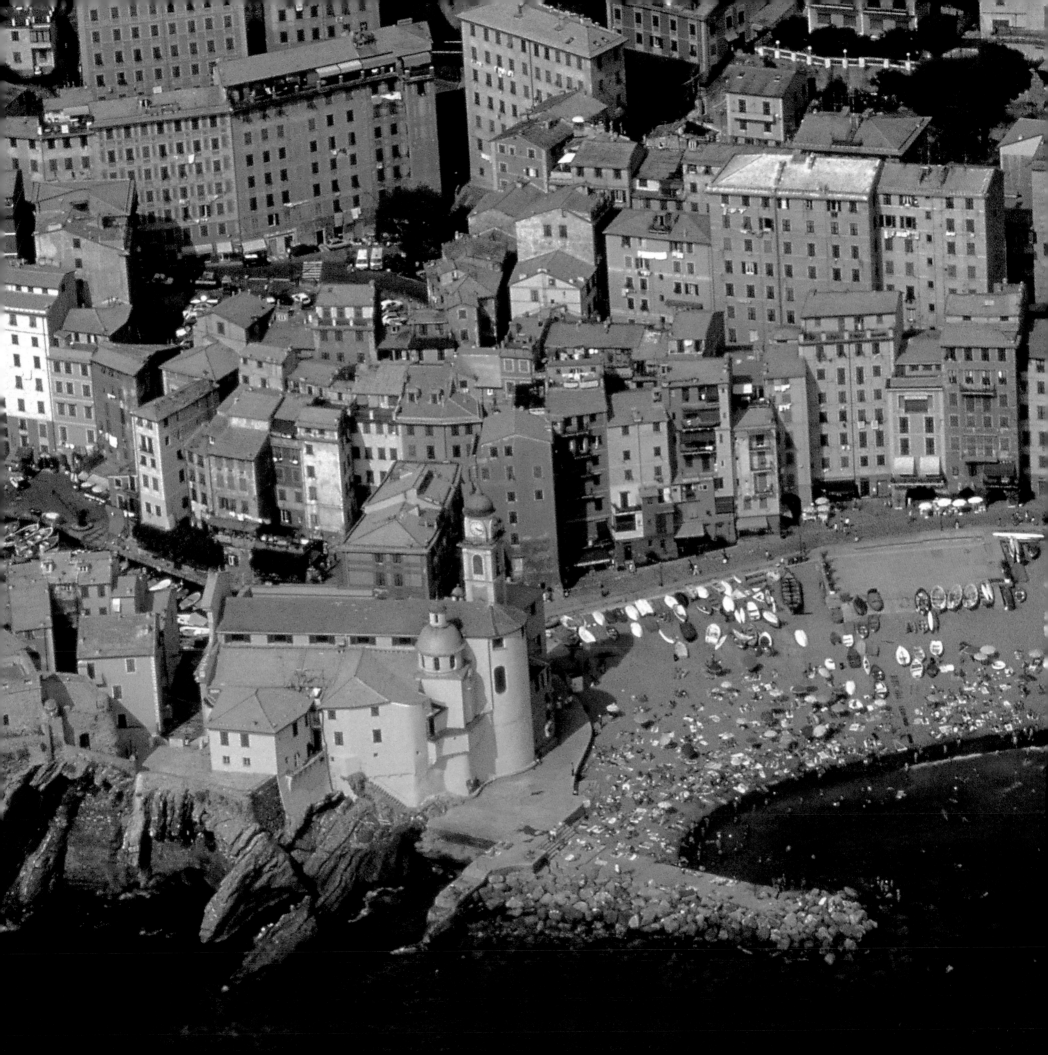

BARCELONA, Spain (left)

Barcelona's Expiatory Temple of the Holy Family, the Sagrada Família, seems to be as much a monument to its architect, Antoni Gaudí i Cornet, as it is to God. Gaudí worked on it from 1891 until his death in 1926, and he is buried in the crypt. Since then, the cathedral has come on in fits and starts. A local sculptor, Josep M. Subirachs, has embellished the near "Passion" façade; a Japanese, Etsuro Sotoo, has added to the façade opposite.

CHÂTEAU DE CLERMONT, Loire, France (below)

Château de Clermont is a privately owned castle in the air. It is at Le Cellier in the Loire on the site of the former Chapel of Clermont and was built by René Chenu de Clermont in 1649. He was governor of two other châteaux, a minister for the prince of Condé and advisor to the king. His seigneurial rights at Le Cellier extended beyond the château to the surrounding villages. Life here was sufficiently exciting to attract the attention of the brilliant seventeenth-century writer Madame de Sévigné.

STROMBOLI, Italy

About 400 people live on this constantly
active volcanic cone. Known as the
Black Giant, Stromboli is the most
northerly of the seven Lipari islands to the
north of Sicily and west of Italy's toe.
The rumbles are ceaseless, and the
eruptions light the night sky and pour
glowing lava into the sea.

THE DUOMO, Milan, Italy (left)

An "imitation hedgehog" is how the English novelist D.H. Lawrence described the Duomo in Milan. At the heart of the city it is one of Europe's largest churches, and was founded with the gift of a marble quarry, which it has kept. The stone has been sculpted into some 2250 statues to add to the 135 pinnacles. The cathedral inspired builders for nearly 500 years, starting in 1386.

VENCE, France (right)

What drew Matisse, Picasso and Rouault to the Côte d'Azur was not just the blue sea, but the medieval hilltop villages within easy reach among the hills behind. They all stayed here, in Vence, between Nice and Antibes, though they would never have had such a view of it as this. At the center, the tower of the Romanesque church stares up at the distant Alps, while around it, like a great skirt, the streets swirl in a giddy circle until they reach the ravines at its sides.

THE COLOSSEUM, Rome, Italy

The whole panoply of Rome's empire is
evoked in the Colosseum. The Eternal City's
most enduring monument, built for the
first plebeian emperor, Vespasian, was
inaugurated in AD 80. On the first day 5000
wild animals were killed to amuse the
spectators. The building was faced with
marble and stucco, and awnings kept the
sun from the audience's critical eyes.

LA DÉFENSE, Paris, France (left)

The Arc de Triomphe has the biggest picture frame in the world. The Grand Arch at La Défense, one of Paris's monumental buildings of the 1980s, rises in the west of the city where it is a window on the modern finance and business district. Designed by Johan Otto von Spreckelsen, it is 361 feet (110 meters) high and 328 feet (100 meters) wide.

SEVILLE, Spain (right)

The immense size of the cathedral in Seville is not always appreciated; it is one of the largest in Christendom. It was built from 1401 to 1507 on the site of a mosque, which bequeathed its Patio de los Naranjos (Orange-Tree Courtyard), seen on the far side, and its minaret.

SAN GIMIGNANO, Italy

The thirteen skyscrapers of San Gimignano in Tuscany are all that remain of no less than 76 which grew out of this wealthy medieval town. Families built them so they could hurl stones down on their enemies; and to show off, they tried to top their neighbor's towers. Finally, the authorities, fearful that the People's Palace (in the center of the photograph) might itself be surpassed, restricted their height to 177 feet (54 meters).

POMPEII, Italy (left)

Until 24 August AD 79, Pompeii was a bustling place of shops, bars and taverns. Its main road, Via di Stabia (seen here), led to the sunny colonnaded marketplace. But when Vesuvius's volcano erupted on that summer's day, the town and one-tenth of its 20 000 citizens were buried in lava and ash.

CÁDIZ, Spain (right)

When the Guadalquivir silted up in the eighteenth century Cádiz took over from Seville as southern Spain's principal port for Atlantic shipping. Trade with South America brought it temporary wealth which it expended, among other things, on its domed cathedral.

LE JARDIN DES PLANTES,
Paris, France

Located near the Paris Mosque, the public
garden and the botanic garden contain
about 5000 varieties of plants, trees and
flowers. The botanic garden was the
passion of Jean-Baptiste Callard de la
Ducquerie who, in 1689, began the
collection with plants from his private
park. The gardens were expanded in the
eighteenth century and following the
French Revolution they were opened to the
public. Mosaics made from flowers and
unusual landscaping, such as this spiral
hedge, are found throughout the garden.

THE ISLANDERS

UNITED KINGDOM ∽ REPUBLIC OF IRELAND

Famously wet and windy between the North Sea and the Atlantic Ocean, the British Isles are perhaps the most fateful of all the world's islands, and they stand in a unique relationship to the rest of Europe. Four nations occupy these relatively uninviting islands— the English, the Irish, the Welsh and the Scots—and they are grouped into two states: 59 million people live in the United Kingdom of Great Britain and Northern Ireland, three and a half million live in the Republic of Ireland, and the mutual attitudes of the two are notoriously equivocal. The islands have not been occupied by an outside power since AD 1066, and for several centuries they have been governed, in one degree or another, by systems of parliamentary democracy.

Most of the land is good agricultural country, well-watered and easy. But in the west and in the north—in Wales, in much of Scotland, along the Atlantic shore of Ireland— rough highlands predominate, and this accentuates the chief ethnic division of the population, between the Anglo-Saxon, deriving from Teutonic invaders who arrived in the Christian era, and the Celtic, descended from far earlier waves of Mediterranean immigration. It was here that the Roman empire reached its final frontier. The legions never controlled northern Scotland, and they never crossed the Irish Sea. The archipelago was an extremity of the Roman world then, and it remains an extremity of Europe still, never quite assimilated into the European consciousness.

Several of Europe's great historical trends, nevertheless, are epitomized in the British Isles. The continent's ancient dynastic fervors survive here in a rich and ostentatious monarchy. The feudalism that once dominated Europe finds its mementos still in the obtrusive class system of England

BODIAM CASTLE, Sussex, England, United Kingdom

This medieval fortress, located on the river Rother, was built by Sir Edward Dalyngrygge between 1385 and 1390 to protect the Rother Valley against invasion by the French. The castle was damaged during the English Civil War and remained empty for years after. In the early twentieth century Lord Curzon purchased the castle and began a program of rebuilding and restoration.

and in the kilts, tartans and rituals of the Scottish clans. The religious struggles of the continent survive here in a violent, apparently insoluble and almost stylized conflict between Catholics and Protestants in Northern Ireland. Europe's instinct for aggression and expansion has found some of its most vigorous exponents among these islanders—from the sixteenth century to the twentieth the British were engaged in a career of overseas acquisition which made them briefly the most powerful people on earth, ruling territories in every continent and brazenly commanding all the oceans.

LLANGYNOG VALLEY,
Wales, United Kingdom

Llangynog Valley is in the heart of northern Wales, between the English border and Snowdonia National Park. The language of the people here is more often Welsh than English. Trapped in the valley, where the sun's shadow moves like the ebb and flow of the tide, are the small fields of the farmers. But there is no sign of the ponies that are bred for people to trot over the hills for their holidays.

Above all, it was here that Europe first mechanized itself, when the power of steam was harnessed by British scientists and engineers at the end of the eighteenth century. The mastery of this technique not only made the British wealthy, but it made them primarily an urban nation—the first in Europe. Today England in particular is one of the most crowded of all countries, and the vast city of London, sprawled in the southeast corner of the islands in a welter of suburbs and problems, epitomizes urban life.

The British attitude to Europe remains ambivalent. No other European power is an island state, and none has looked so instinctively to the sea for its fortunes. For centuries the British tried to stay clear of continental involvements, intervening only when it seemed that one European power or another was becoming dangerously dominant. Now their empire has gone, and their industrial capacity has long been overtaken, but their overseas investments are still enormous, and many older citizens still feel they have more in

BRADFORD, Yorkshire, England, United Kingdom (left)

This is a suburb to provoke identity crises: redbrick rows, slate-roofed and serried, with the occasional attic dormer window struggling for a view above the rest. There is nothing to suggest that this is Bradford, Yorkshire's wool and textile city of dark satanic mills. Nor, in these unpeopled side streets, is there anything to convey the city's large Asian population, or the achievements of its inspired sons, such as the artist David Hockney.

THE SOUTH DOWNS,
England, United Kingdom (below)

The rolling chalk ridges of the South Downs come to an abrupt halt when they reach the English Channel around Eastbourne. The cliff face comprises seven hills, known as the Seven Sisters, divided by the valleys of former rivers.

common with the other English-speaking peoples, scattered across the world, than with their continental neighbors.

In 1990 the British Isles were linked for the first time by a tunnel to France. Most Europeans thought this was another step in the islands' inevitable absorption into a pan-European system. Old-school Britons, though, remembered with nostalgia a much-loved, frequently quoted but actually apocryphal headline from *The Times* of London: *Violent Storms in the English Channel, Continent Isolated.*

OXFORD, England, United Kingdom

Gothic spires rise above the halls and quadrangles of Oxford University's 30 colleges. The Radcliffe Camera, the country's first circular library, built in 1748, is to the left of the steeple of St Mary's Church. Below it is the lantern-topped semicircle of Sir Christopher Wren's Sheldonian Theatre.

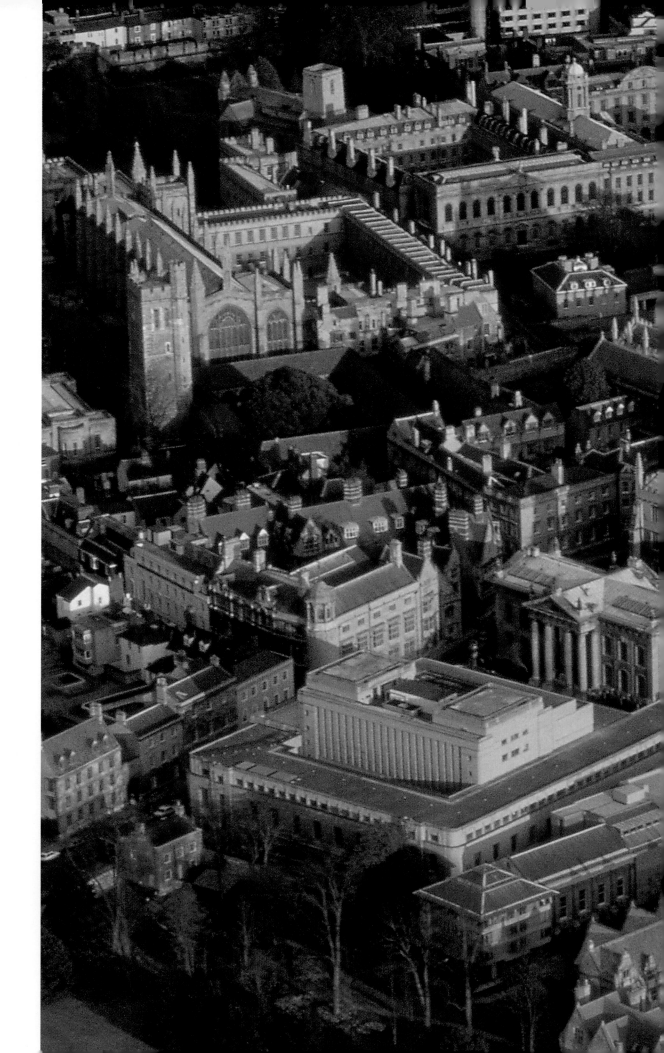

CAERNARFON CASTLE, Wales, United Kingdom (below)

Apart from the cars and the yachts, Caernarfon Castle, on the north coast of Wales, looks much as it must have done when it was built by Edward I following England's conquest of the principality in 1282. Edward's heir was crowned Prince of Wales in the castle, a practice continued right up until today; Prince Charles was invested with the title in a ceremony here in 1969.

INISHMAAN, Aran Islands, Republic of Ireland (right)

On the west coast of Ireland, forming a natural breakwater across Galway Bay, are the three Aran Islands. This is Inishmaan, between Inisheer and Inishmore. These "ancient islands of the saints" are peopled by Gaelic-speaking fishermen and farmers. Inishmaan has also attracted such creative talents as John Millington Synge, who was inspired here to write *The Playboy of the Western World*.

THE WHITE HORSE, Oxfordshire, England, United Kingdom

This gigantic figure is located on the eponymous Whitehorse Hill near Uffington in Oxfordshire. The 374-foot (114-meter) long horse was created by cutting turf out of the hillside to expose the chalky soil underneath. It is believed the horse is the oldest hill figure in the United Kingdom. It was carved during prehistoric times but exactly when and the purpose of the figure remain unknown.

ST PAUL'S CATHEDRAL, London, United Kingdom (left)

Sir Christopher Wren could only imagine this view of his greatest work. St Paul's Cathedral is London's fifth church on Ludgate Hill. A mixture of baroque and classical, it was completed after 36 years in 1710 and was the first purpose-built Protestant cathedral in England. Its cruciform shape is laid out beneath the 365-foot (110-meter) stone cupola, lantern, ball and cross, around which external galleries provide an elevated view of the city. A Latin inscription on Wren's burial place in the crypt says: "Reader, if you seek his monument, look around you."

PORTHMADOG, Wales, United Kingdom (right)

The river Glaslyn in north Wales is a place for men of vision. William Alexander Maddocks built Porthmadog in the 1820s for the export of slate brought down from Snowdonia. In the 1920s the architect Sir Clough Williams-Ellis built the neighboring fantasy Italianate village of Portmeirion.

BLENHEIM PALACE, Oxfordshire,
England, United Kingdom

A grateful country gave part of the
Oxfordshire countryside to John Churchill,
Duke of Marlborough, for his military
successes in the War of the Spanish
Succession, notably at Blenheim in Bavaria,
after which this estate was named. The
building was designed by Sir John
Vanbrugh in 1705 and is set in landscaped
grounds. In 1874 one of the family home's
200 rooms echoed to the first cries of the
infant Winston Churchill.

OXFORDSHIRE, England,
United Kingdom (left)

Near Witney, Oxfordshire, a tributary of
the Windrush meanders through a stand
of fresh-leafed poplars, interrupting their
perfectly ordered lines.

TRINITY COLLEGE, Dublin,
Republic of Ireland (right)

The great quadrangles of Trinity College,
Dublin, focus on a 100-foot (30-meter)
campanile erected in 1853 on the site of
the medieval monastery church the college
replaced when it was built in 1591. Among
the treasures in its library is the beautiful
late-eighth-century illuminated
manuscript, the *Book of Kells*. Beyond the
university is the curved façade of the Bank
of Ireland, begun in 1729 to house the
parliament. O'Connell Bridge leads across
the river Liffey to the city's north side.

EDINBURGH,
Scotland, United Kingdom

The afternoon sun is too weak to melt
Edinburgh's snow. On the rock is the city's
first building, its castle. The hill slopes
down to the right along the Royal Mile and
into the medieval old town. Princes Street
cuts the scene in half horizontally, dividing
the straggling old town from New Town's
neat Georgian crescents and squares.

IRON BRIDGE, Shropshire,
England, United Kingdom (left)

It is hard to think of this sparkling gorge
on the river Severn in Shropshire as the
birthplace of the Industrial Revolution.
But near here in 1709 Abraham Darby first
smelted iron using coke as fuel. Seventy
years later his grandson designed this
bridge, the first in the world to be made
of cast iron.

CARDIFF ARMS PARK, Cardiff,
Wales, United Kingdom (right)

Offically called Millennium Stadium, this
arena is more popularly known as Cardiff
Arms Park. This sporting ground is home
for the national rugby team. The Welsh are
passionate supporters of that particular
football code. The stadium was completed
in 1999 in time for the Rugby World Cup.

STONEHENGE, Salisbury Plain,
England, United Kingdom

Stonehenge has stood on Salisbury Plain
for about 4000 years. Nobody knows
exactly why the massive stones, weighing
up to 50 tons (51 tonnes), were brought
from Wales; or why they were erected in
two concentric circles with a horseshoe
shape within.

FOUNTAINS ABBEY, Yorkshire, United Kingdom (left)

This Cistercian abbey, founded in the early twelfth century, was for a time one of the richest religious houses in England. Following Henry VIII's Dissolution of the Monasteries bill in 1539, the abbey was closed and fell into disrepair. The ruins of Fountains Abbey are now within the grounds of Studley Royal Park.

LONDON, England, United Kingdom (right)

This is a familiar face of London: the clock above Westminster Palace, the seat of Britain's government since the eleventh century. From here the sound of the hour being struck by its largest bell, the $13^1/_2$-ton (13.7-tonne) Big Ben, is deafening.

PENTLAND HILLS,
Scotland, United Kingdom

This collection of small hills is located
just to the south of Edinburgh. The area
is a popular place for hiking, horse riding
and picnicking. On a clear day the views
from here stretch to Edinburgh and the
coast of Fife.

KILMACDUAGH, County Galway, Republic of Ireland (left)

Worn to the color of the dry bones in the graveyard that surrounds it, the ruins of the monastery at Kilmacduagh near Gort, County Galway, seem entombed by time. These are some of the remains of the ecclesiastical see founded by St Colman Macduagh in the seventh century. Still standing is a 112-foot (34-meter) tower, leaning 25 inches (64 centimeters) out of perpendicular.

SALISBURY PLAIN, England, United Kingdom (right)

There is a haunting emptiness about Salisbury Plain in southwest England. There are prehistoric burial grounds here, earthworks, camps and stone circles, all evidence of early settlements. Yet since then, no villages have grown up and there have been no real signs of life. The undulating chalk plain is 20 miles (32 kilometers) long and about 500 feet (152 meters) above sea level. In 1897 the government began to buy up the land for military use; what remains is planted principally with crops.

HAMPTON COURT PALACE,
England, United Kingdom

In the early 16th century Thomas, Cardinal Wolsey obtained the lease to this manor house located on the river Thames and transformed it into an opulent Tudor palace. Wolsey, who had been Henry VIII's chief minister, gave this estate to the king. Henry VIII significantly extended and rebuilt the palace. Subsequent monarchs changed the buildings very little, until William III and Mary II commissioned Sir Christopher Wren to remodel the palace in the late 17th century. At this time the gardens were also significantly altered and the famous maze was added. The innovations introduced by William III form the basis of the present garden, seen here.

ALBERT MEMORIAL, London, England, United Kingdom (left)

This memorial in Kensington Gardens was built to honor Prince Albert, the consort of Queen Victoria. The monument, designed by Sir George Gilbert Scott, was completed in 1872. A statue of Prince Albert stands in the center of the 175-foot (53-meter) memorial. To the south of Kensington Gardens is the Royal Albert Hall, another, more functional tribute to Prince Albert.

BRIGHTON'S PALACE PIER, England, United Kingdom (right)

Britain's traditional seasides, of bracing promenades and family fun, are evoked by their piers, and the best known is Brighton's Palace Pier, defying the waves 1640 feet (500 meters) out to sea. In 1823 the country's first, Chain Pier, was built here, and it served as a jetty for a ferry crossing to Dieppe in France. After a storm brought it down in 1896, the Palace Pier was built to replace it.

COUNTY SLIGO, Republic of Ireland

This great velvet pincushion is "bare Ben Bulben's head," a 1730-foot (527-meter) mountain between Sligo and Donegal Bay. This part of Ireland was the haunt of the Nobel poet laureate W.B. Yeats (1865–1939) and his artist brother, Jack. Though the poet died in the south of France, his body was returned here to the churchyard at the foot of Ben Bulben.

INISHMORE,
Aran Islands, Republic of Ireland (below)

Inishmore is about 16 square miles (41 sq km) and the largest of the three arid, limestone Aran Islands. The island has a rich archaeological heritage, including two megalithic tombs. There are thousands of stone walls, like these near the castle ruins, all over the island.

PALACE OF WESTMINSTER,
London, England, United Kingdom (right)

The Houses of Parliament, known as the Palace of Westminster, sit next to Big Ben on the river Thames. The House of Commons and the House of Lords are both located here. The complex was designed by Sir Charles Barry in the Gothic Revival style and built between 1837 and 1860.

YORK MINSTER, York,
England, United Kingdom

The Cathedral of St Peter in York is the largest Gothic church in Britain. In the early thirteenth century the Archbishop of York, Walter de Gray, determined to build a cathedral to rival Canterbury. Construction began in 1220 and continued for the next 250 years. Today York Minster dominates the center of York.

LONDON EYE, London,
England, United Kingdom (left)

At 450 feet (140 meters) high, this observation wheel was the highest in the world when it opened in early 2000. The Eye is located on the south bank of the river Thames opposite Big Ben and the Houses of Parliament. From the top there are spectacular views of the Thames and central London.

LOCH ECK, Scotland,
United Kingdom (right)

This is the essential Scotland of uncompromising mountains, deep narrow lochs, and roads that wind through sparsely inhabited glens. Loch Eck, 6 miles (10 kilometers) long, lies to the southwest of the kingdom. On the left is Glenbranter Forest, on the right Beinn Mhór, high points of the 60 000-acre (24 280-hectare) Argyll Forest Park. In the glen below, the road leads to the Younger Botanic Garden at Benmore, part of Edinburgh's Royal Botanical Garden.

DURHAM CATHEDRAL, Durham, England, United Kingdom

Situated on this peninsula in the river Wear are Durham Cathedral and Castle. Construction on the Norman cathedral began in 1093 and continued for about 200 years. Located behind the cathedral is Durham Castle which William the Conqueror ordered built. The castle was a defense against invasion by the Scots from the north.

THE NORTHERNERS

SWEDEN ∽ NORWAY ∽ DENMARK ∽ FINLAND ∽ ICELAND

Together with Denmark, the Nordic countries of Norway, Sweden, Finland, Iceland, the Faeroes and Åland form more than a geographical unit. No other such group of European states constitutes a more organic company—ethnically, historically, politically, religiously, artistically and even temperamentally. When somebody speaks of a Scandinavian, an instant stereotype is summoned into almost all our minds.

These countries of the north are mostly ungenerous of terrain, mountainous, sparse and forested. Only Denmark and southern Sweden offer rich pasture land, and Scandinavians have traditionally been obliged to earn their living in tough vocations—as fishermen, seamen, lumbermen or graziers. Coupled with a

paucity of winter sunshine, or even daylight, this has made for those characteristics of strength, taciturnity, introspection and sudden exuberance that the whole world recognizes.

Nobody knows the origins of the Sami, or Lapps, who live in the extreme north of Sweden, Finland and Norway, sometimes nomadically with reindeer. The Finns evidently originated somewhere in the east. The others, however, are quintessentially Nordic. Except again for the Finns, whose language is akin to Hungarian, they all speak a variety of the same Germanic language. At one time or another most of them have occupied each others' territories or have formed part of the

VÄXJÖ, Sweden

Typical domestic architecture around Växjö, the county town of Kronoberg, southern Sweden. The
woodlands provide much of the region's industry—manufacturing furniture, paper and matches.
But this area is also known as the "Kingdom of Glass" because of its seventeen major glassworks.
The techniques were introduced to the country by Gustavus I, who brought the idea from Bohemia.

same state—even Iceland was constitutionally subject to Denmark until 1944—and this has given them similar styles of government. The Scandinavian countries (Norway, Sweden and Denmark) have monarchies of the most self-effacing kind. Their kings and queens generally prefer populist activities to great parades, and all the Nordic states are governed by staunchly democratic systems. Iceland claims to have the oldest elected assembly on earth, the Altiing having been in existence, except for a hiatus in the nineteenth century, for more than a thousand years.

A streak of the heroic runs through these societies. This was the homeland of the Vikings, the bravos of medieval Europe, whose trading settlements extended as far as the eastern Mediterranean, who reconnoitered Greenland and North America, and whose occupation of Normandy (Norseman's land) led to the conquest of England. The characteristics of a fighting aristocracy, though muffled in Scandinavia now, are remembered always through those great works of medieval literature, the Icelandic

SMÖGEN, Sweden

The white houses of Smögen give the island a clean and healthy holiday air. Along the quayside tourists browse in the shops and admire the boats in one of Sweden's most popular sailing resorts. The fishing is good here and shrimp are a particular favorite. Smögen is north of Göteborg and is connected to the mainland by a 1320-foot (403-meter) bridge.

Sagas, which record the high-flown
pugnacity of the Norwegian kings
dwelling in Iceland, and the exploits
of legendary heroes.

In modern times the Scandinavians
have been among the least
aggressive of European countries,
devoting themselves chiefly to
social progress and enrichment.
They were relatively unharmed by
the great twentieth-century wars,
and have been famous pioneers
of public welfare and successful
economic specialists: the Danes
as agriculturists; the Norwegians
as shipowners; the Swedes as
manufacturers of cars, aircraft and
machinery; the Finns as lumbermen
and shipbuilders. In the European
context they have been successful
chiefly in cooperating among
themselves. Long before Europe
began its movement toward unity,
the Scandinavian countries had
established common institutions
of their own and had managed to
present themselves to the world as
a bloc—the first to prove, despite
all the historical evidence, that
Europeans need not be endemically
at each others' throats.

FREDERIKSBORG CASTLE, Denmark (left)

The skyline of Frederiksborg Castle is thoroughly pricked by the gleaming, spiked-helmet roof of its Gatehouse Tower and other well-honed architectural points. Built on three islands in a small lake near Hillerød on Zealand at the beginning of the seventeenth century, the castle is seen as the pinnacle of Denmark's renaissance. Although named after King Frederick II, who built an earlier castle here, it was his son, Christian IV, who was responsible for its present size and shape. It now houses a museum of national history.

SMÅLAND, Sweden (above)

Harvest time in Småland, southern Sweden, where the hay is kept dry in plastic wrapping. The region looks prosperous now, but in the nineteenth century poor agriculture and a booming population meant Småland accounted for a fifth of Sweden's one million emigrants to the United States. At the nearby town of Växjö there is a House of Emigrants which has a museum and the largest archives on the subject in Europe.

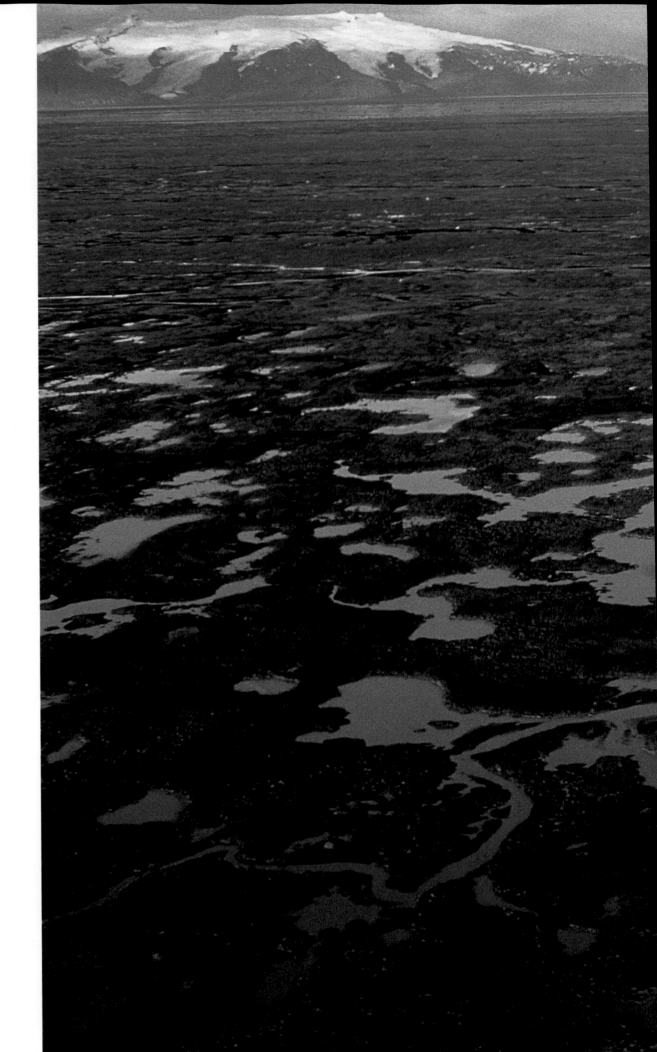

SKEIDHARÁRSANDUR, Iceland

This remote, chilly spot is Skeidharársandur in southern Iceland. Boulders and debris have been brought here by a concentration of glacial flows originating in Iceland's largest glacier. Underground thermal and volcanic activity makes the region unpredictable and uninhabitable, and the lack of foxes and other animals makes it a safe breeding ground for gulls. Until a bridge was built here in 1976, drivers taking the coastal road had to take a 155-mile (250-kilometer) detour around the region to continue 30 miles (50 kilometers) further along the coast.

COPENHAGEN, Denmark (below)

There is a pleasant openness about the Amalienborg
Palace in Copenhagen, with its generous octagonal
square approached from four sides. The palace's four
wings were originally separate noble houses. Two
wings are now occupied by Queen Margrethe II and
her family.

LAKE SAIMAA, Finland (right)

Timber, pulp, cardboard, paper . . . these are the exports that keep
Finland afloat. About one-tenth of the country is covered by its 60 000
lakes; most of the rest is covered by coniferous trees. The felled logs
are transported many miles through a network of rivers and lakes. Lake
Saimaa covers 500 square miles (1300 square kilometers) and is the
most southerly part of the system.

ÅLESUND, Norway

Ålesund is a town that spills out across
the sea, occupying three of the islands
or skerries that are liberally scattered all
along Norway's west coast. Although an
ancient town and one of the country's
main fishing ports, none of the old wooden
architecture remains. This was replaced by
stone buildings after a catastrophic fire in
1904. Thus the church, seen on the middle
island of Aspøya, dates from 1909, and
many houses are enriched with touches
of Art Nouveau.

GAMLA UPPSALA, Sweden (left)

These three artificial hillocks may be the last resting place of kings Adil, Egil and Aun. They are the largest of a group of burial mounds in Gamla (Old) Uppsala, the ancient home of Sweden's kings just north of Uppsala. Dating from about AD 500, the *Folkvandringstiden* or "time of migration" that preceded the Viking era, the mounds lie along a natural ridge beside the parish church built on the site of Scandinavia's last pagan temple.

STOCKHOLM, Sweden (right)

Sweden's capital is splashed across a number of islands afloat on the waters that drain into the Baltic Sea. Stockholm's old town is focused on the island of Staden. The Royal Palace occupies the near right-hand corner; royal weddings and coronations take place in the cathedral just behind; and to their right, on its own island, is the parliament building. Opposite the palace is the National Museum.

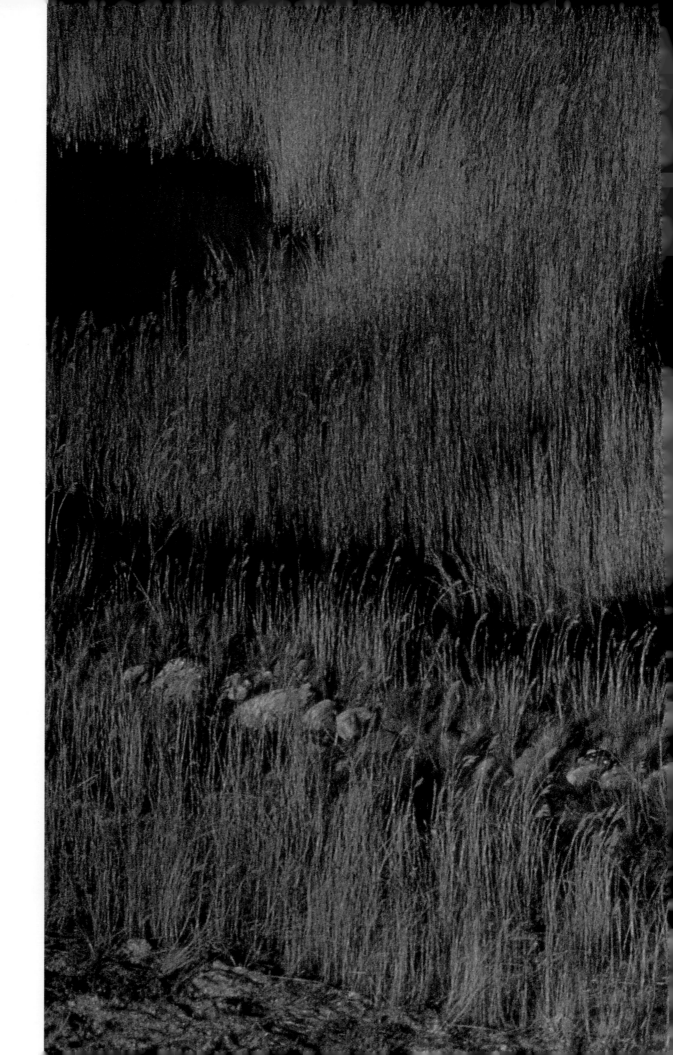

TÅSINGE, Denmark

Surrounded by its own roofing material,
this simple thatched cottage is on the
island of Tåsinge to the south of Fyn,
Denmark's third largest island. This is
a romantic countryside. Buried in a nearby
cemetery are Count Sparre, the Swedish
nobleman, and Elvira Madigan, a tightrope
walker, whose tragic love story from
the nineteenth century was made into a
film in 1967.

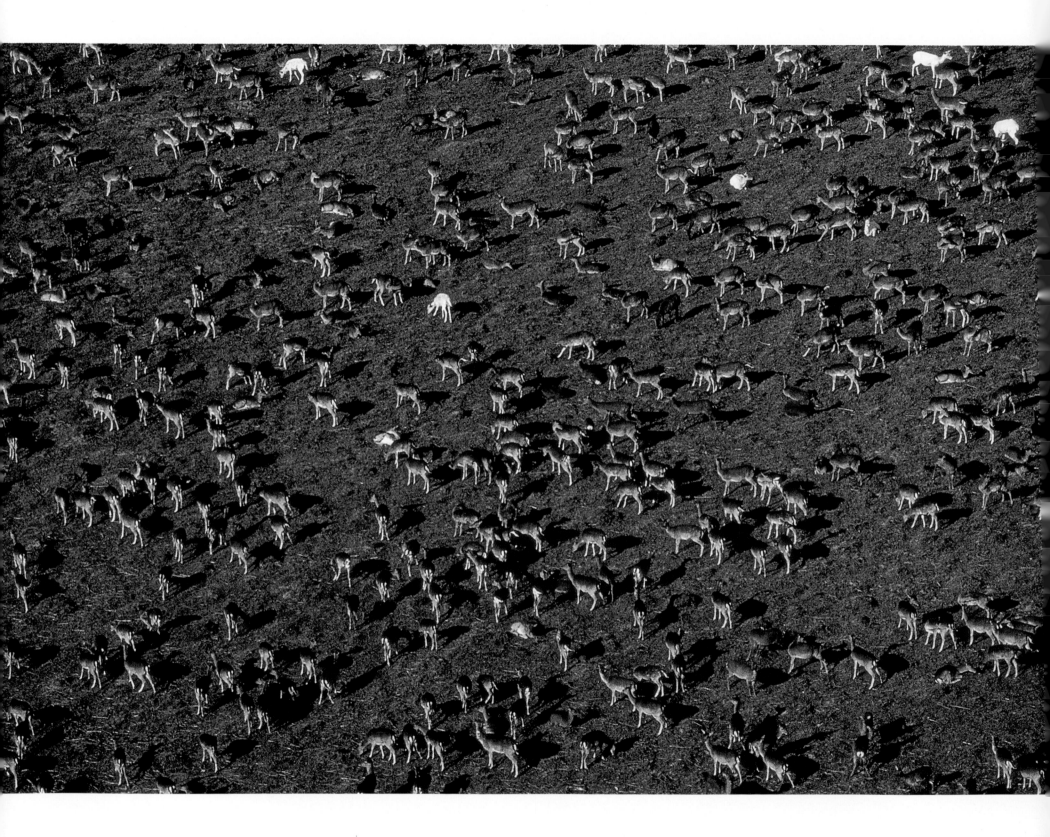

DYREHAVEN, Denmark (left)

A deer herd basks in the sun at Dyrehaven, north of Copenhagen. This large park is popular for walkers, cyclists, horse riders and mushroom gatherers. Adjoining it is a 2500-acre (1000-hectare) beech wood, where a royal hunting lodge, the Ermitage, still functions. On the eastern side of the island of Zealand there are views out across the Øresund to Sweden. On the south side of the park is a popular fairground at Bakken.

REYKJAVÍK, Iceland (right)

What looks like a puff of smoke to the right of the picture is in fact escaped steam, for Reykjavik is officially a smokeless city, with all its heating provided by nearby hot springs. Demand is not excessive. Although situated just on the edge of the Arctic Circle, Iceland has milder winters than New York.

BROENDBY, Copenhagen, Denmark

These are the sort of circles many Danes want to move in. Surrounded by sea, the people of Copenhagen like to go inland, to appreciate the flat, fertile island of Zealand. Allotment gardens are a common sight throughout Scandinavia, and here in the suburb of Broendby, just south of the capital, people can find a slice of country life. Planned with great formality, each garden is 4375 square feet (400 square meters), and each chalet is 440 square feet (40 square meters). There are 500 gardens in all.

KRONBORG CASTLE, Denmark (left)

This is where Shakespeare set the opening scene of his great tragedy, *Hamlet*, in the port which in Danish is called Helsingør. The castle is Kronborg, and it was completed a dozen years or so before Shakespeare wrote his play.

JOSTEDALSBREEN GLACIER, Norway (right)

Jostedalsbreen in western Norway is mainland Europe's largest snowfield, covering about 340 square miles (880 square kilometers). The ice can be up to 1650 feet (500 meters) deep, though it is gradually retreating.

ØSTERBRO, Copenhagen, Denmark

Built in the 1890s, these rows of houses
are called Kartoffelraekkerne (potato rows)
or English style, referring to the acres of
terraced housing that went up around the
industrial cities of England in the
nineteenth century.

ÖLAND BRIDGE, Sweden (left)

The Öland Bridge in Sweden takes traffic up and over the Kalmarsund from the mainland town of Kalmar and delivers it to Möllstorp on the island of Öland in the Baltic Sea. Built in 1972, the bridge is more that 3 miles (6 kilometers) from shore to shore, with 153 piers. It has increased the popularity of this long, narrow and rather flat island as a holiday resort. Among its attractions are Viking rune stones, forts and nearly 400 windmills.

UPPSALA, Sweden (right)

Uppsala's tidy, symmetrical cathedral is Sweden's largest church and its towers rise 390 feet (119 meters). It was consecrated in 1435 and given its northern Gothic look by a French architect, Etienne de Bonneuil. Gustavus I (1496–1560), founder of modern Sweden, is buried here, and so is Linneaus (1707–78), founder of modern botany. The old university town of Uppsala is also the see of the Lutheran Archbishop of Sweden.

LAKE INARI, Finland

Way up in the north of Finland, on the edge of Norway and the Russian Federation, is Inari, a lake as big as an inland sea. Some 3000 islands are scattered around its clear, still waters, and until the nineteenth century they were used by the Lapps as burial places: only here were the departed safe from hungry bears.

THE LOW COUNTRIES

THE NETHERLANDS ∽ BELGIUM ∽ LUXEMBOURG

On the map the Low Countries look as though they are a single state, and once they were. They are the flatlands that surround the North Sea estuaries of three rivers, the Rhine, the Meuse and the Scheldt. At the end of the nineteenth-century Napoleonic wars, after a complex history of dynastic exchange and rivalry, they were briefly united as the Kingdom of the Low Countries. But in the old way of Europe the comity did not last, and they are now divided once more into the kingdoms of Belgium and the Netherlands, and the Grand Duchy of Luxembourg.

They have much in common. They are all small countries—Luxembourg, with an area less than 1000 square miles (about 2600 square kilometers) is the smallest truly independent, sovereign state in Europe. Their histories have often coincided. Their countrysides are almost uniformly flat. Their peoples are all Germanic in origin, and long before the European Common Market came into being they had established their own customs union. Their reputations and destinies, though, have been very different.

Pre-eminent among the three is the Netherlands, more commonly but less officially known as Holland, which has a population of less than 16 million, but has been one of Europe's pace-makers and power-houses. Great sailors, merchants, engineers, patrons and practitioners of art, the Dutch literally created their own country. A quarter of it has been reclaimed from the sea, and it is now the most densely populated state in Europe. From this precarious seashore base, as vulnerable to the elements as it was to enemies from the European interior, the Dutch sailed out to seize for

AMSTERDAM, Netherlands

Amsterdam, capital of the Netherlands, takes its name from the river Amstel, its principal canal.
Tree-lined canals criss-cross this world-renowned city and add considerably to its charm.

themselves one of the biggest of the colonial empires. Even now the Dutch flag flies over several islands of the Caribbean, and the language of the South African Afrikaners is a kind of Dutch. With the spoils of the east they made themselves rich, and they have remained rich by astute trading, by innovative industry, and by exploiting the geographical advantage of their position at the mouth of the Rhine. Huge industries have grown up around the port of Rotterdam—chief outlet to the sea for Germany, and one of the world's busiest seaports—and many Dutch companies are world-wide in their presence.

No such vivid images attach themselves to Belgium, the butt of many jokes from Europeans of a more flamboyant background. Belgium is indeed an unassertive country and well it might be, for nowhere else in Europe has been more cruelly ravaged by the comings and goings of foreign armies. Waterloo is in Belgium, and so is Ypres, and here too are the forests of the Ardennes where Hitler's armies made their last counterattack in the west.

SCHEVENINGEN, Netherlands

The Hague is home to the Dutch parliament and the International Courts of Justice. Just a short tram ride away is Scheveningen on the North Sea. A fashionable resort since the nineteenth century, it has a pier, wide sandy beaches, and the Kurhaus, a hotel with restaurants, bars and casino, which dominates the sea front.

This is Europe's cockpit. Belgium became a nation in 1831, when it was separated from the Netherlands. It is inhabited partly by Flemings of Latin origin, who speak a form of Dutch, and partly by Walloons of Celtic origin, who speak French. Thickly populated, heavily industrialized, producing few things that most of us know about, boasting few heroes that we have heard of, Belgium came justly but paradoxically out of its obscurity when its capital, Brussels, became the administrative headquarters of the European Community and thus a synonym for bureaucracy.

BRUSSELS, Belgium

Belgium's capital, Brussels, is often thought of as the capital of the whole continent of Europe, perhaps because both the European Commission and NATO have their headquarters here. Its earlier glory is reflected in this huge archway, the Cinquantenaire. Attached to it are an aviation museum (bottom left) and the Royal Museums of Art and History (bottom right).

LISSE, Netherlands

Ribbed like corduroy, these Dutch bulb fields near Lisse become bright colored stripes in April and May as tulips come into bloom. Flowers are picked in the evening and auctioned next morning. At Aalsmeer, between Lisse and Amsterdam, millions of plants are sold every day. Nearby, close to Schiphol airport, there are two further auction houses, and flowers can be airfreighted and on sale in most major world cities within 24 hours.

And what of Luxembourg? Oddly enough, for many decades it was a prime symbol of Europeanism. The Grand Duchy was once very much grander, including the whole of what is now Belgium, and it has remained a formidable little state. Its steel production is said to be the highest per capita in the world; it is an eager center of international finance and the legal capital of the European Community. However, what made it seem long ago a supra-European state was the presence there of an international commercial broadcasting industry, transmitting in many languages. In the days when a united Europe seemed no more than a pipedream, the familiar name of Radio Luxembourg carried to listeners far away a first inkling of community.

TEXEL ISLAND, Netherlands

The island of Texel in north Holland is like a flat pancake, with its rim turned up to keep out the tides. On the northern side a long beach is backed by dunes; on the near side a dike holds back the Waddenzee.

GELDERLAND, Netherlands (left)

St Hubert's Hunting Lodge was designed to look like a deer's antlers. It was built for Helene Kröller-Müller, the wife of a shipping magnate, between 1915 and 1920. The lodge was located in their 22-square-mile (57-square-kilometer) estate, now De Hoge Veluwe National Park in Gelderland in the middle of Holland. While here, Mrs Kröller-Müller built up one of the country's finest art collections, still housed in the Kröller-Müller Museum, which she also had built on the estate.

DELFT, Netherlands (right)

In the sixteenth and seventeenth centuries, Delft flourished as a center of Catholic humanism and the arts. One famous son was Hugo Grotius (1583–1645), an early advocate of international law, whose statue is partially hidden by the spire of the New Church.

Moselle River, LUXEMBOURG

A tributary of the Rhine, the Moselle River
forms part of the boundary between
Luxembourg and Germany. For generations
people have used the river to transport
cargo. The opening of the Moselle Canal in
1964 enabled barges up to 1500 tons
(1530 tonnes) in weight to travel along
the waterway.

ANTWERP, Belgium (above)

Antwerp, one of the largest ports in the world, lies on the river Schelde in Belgium, 55 miles (88 kilometers) from the North Sea. It was the home of Peter Paul Rubens (1577–1640) whose masterpiece, a triptych called *Descent from the Cross*, is housed in the Gothic Cathedral of Our Lady.

WATERLOO, Belgium (right)

On this Belgian field on June 18, 1815, modern Europe's most ambitious and talented general was finally defeated. At Waterloo Napoléon Bonaparte, emperor of France, was trounced in a two-day battle by allied forces under Britain's Duke of Wellington and Prussia's von Blücher. This commemorative statue of a lion marks the spot where the 23-year-old Prince of Orange, son of William I of the Netherlands, was wounded in the shoulder.

ROTTERDAM, Netherlands (above)

This is the world's largest and busiest port. Rotterdam is 19 miles (30 kilometers) upriver from the North Sea and Europoort, where major petroleum companies have refining facilities. Through the city runs the Nieuwe Maas, spanned here by the red Willems Bridge. Its waterways connect with the Rhine and lead into the heart of industrial Germany. Heavy bombing in the Second World War has meant the city is largely of modern design, though a very small part of the old port remains, visible in the top left of the picture.

ESCH-SUR-SÛRE, Luxembourg (left)

A meander in the twinkling river Sûre forms an almost complete moat around the medieval castle of Esch-sur-Sûre in Luxembourg. At night the ruins of the tenth-century fort and the church in front of it are floodlit, making it one of the Grand Duchy's special attractions. The town is in the north of the small country, in the forest of the Ardennes.

THE HEARTLANDS

GERMANY ∽ AUSTRIA ∽ SWITZERLAND

In the very heart of Europe, at the center of its preoccupations for hundreds of years, lies a language—German—the language of Goethe and Schiller, Beethoven and Martin Luther, of Einstein and Benz, of Adolf Hitler. The energies of this powerful tongue, which inspires a particular loyalty among all who use it, have frequently governed the course of history and bind these territories together not only linguistically but also in style and often in emotion.

It is true that in one of the states of this Germanic core, Switzerland, three other national languages are also officially recognized—French, Italian and Romansh—but then Switzerland, which is not even a member of the United Nations, stands outside every norm, in its wealth, beauty, complacency and conservatism, as in its constitutional neutrality. Austria too is *sui generis* as a state, being the rump of the once-mighty Habsburg empire. And Liechtenstein is only just a state, for its foreign affairs, its defense, its postal services and even its currencies are managed by the Swiss.

But Germany itself, the cradle of the language, exerts such powerful suggestions and has played so important and sometimes terrible a part in the history of the twentieth century, that its status has become almost a metaphor for the destiny of Europe. When in 1990 its two halves were reunited after thirty years of Cold War alienation, this event more than any other seemed to carry the promise of a Europe reconciled; for without a strong, stable and peaceable Germany at its center, the idea of Europe loses its potency.

SALZBURG, Austria

Salzburg, birthplace of Mozart and one of Europe's most musical cities, lies silent in the snow. In the background is the shadowy bulk of the Hohensalzburg fortress, dating mainly from 1500. Below it the sun catches the seventeenth-century towers of the west front of the cathedral. The angular building on this side of it, centered on three large marble courtyards, is the palace of the prince-bishops who ruled from the thirteenth century. Mozart was born in a house between here and the Salzach River.

It is a relative newcomer among the nation-states, as it is among the democracies. Split for centuries into fissiparous principalities, disrupted again by the sixteenth-century Reformation which was later to divide all Europe, addled by countless wars and dynastic settlements, it became a modern unified state only in 1871. Even into the twentieth century Prussians, Saxons and Bavarians hardly recognized themselves as the same nationality, for all their common heritage of language. Even now Germany remains a federation of disparate provinces.

TOWN HALL, Munich, Germany

Marienplatz is the heart of the Bavarian capital of Munich. Here is where people meet, to sit out at the café tables or in the beer halls. Rising beside them on a small plinth is a gold statue of the Virgin Mary (erected 1638), after whom the square is named. The ornate white tower looking down over it belongs to the nineteenth-century town hall. Twice a day its clock chimes, and mechanical figures come out to dance.

OFFINGEN, Germany

The village of Offingen in Upper Swabia, south of Stuttgart, pulls a blanket of hoarfrost around itself as the faint sun of a January dawn tries to prise it from sleep. Blue with cold, the wooded hillside of Bussen encircles the church dedicated to Our Lady of Sorrow. This Gothic building was founded in 1516, and attracts a number of pilgrims every year.

Many kinds of terrain are to be found in this microcosm of the continent. There are Baltic ports and North Sea beaches; there are the Alps of Bavaria and the forests of Baden-Württemberg; Hamburg, in the northwest, is a famously liberal and outward-looking seaport, with old British connections; Munich, in the southeast, is a paradigm of German continentalism, close to Switzerland, Austria, Italy and the Czech Republic. The eastern provinces, so long stifled by communism, struggle with economic and social disadvantage; in the west the cult of materialism is to be seen at its glitziest and most successful.

LÜBECK, Germany

Lübeck, "Queen of the Hansa," was the capital of the Hanseatic League of trading towns that stretched from the Netherlands to Poland, monopolizing trade across the Baltic to Russia and Scandinavia. The brick-built town arose on an island on the River Trave and could be approached through the sturdy Holstentor, the twin round-towered gate in the medieval walls seen on the bottom left. On the right are the twin towers of St Mary's, completed in 1330 for the city burghers.

For the most part the Germanic peoples have concerned themselves with Europe, their excursions into colonialism having been brief and limited. The work of their geniuses has of course become part of the world's cultural inheritance. Mozart and Freud seem to be compatriots of us all yet their language remains almost symbolically European. And Berlin, more than any other European city, exemplifies the mixed significance of this continent. Standing more or less at its epicenter it has become, thanks to Adolf Hitler, a place of evil memory. Nevertheless, reunited as it is around the fulcrum of the Brandenburg Gate, with its equivocal emanations of tragedy, merriment, new hope and a lingering distrust, it has become once again the natural capital of Europe.

HALLE, Germany

Postwar planning in the German Democratic Republic left the Paulus Church (1903) the focal point of a suburban district of the industrial city of Halle, northwest of Leipzig. The town was first mentioned in a document dating from AD 806, referring to fortifications to be built around saline springs that for many centuries gave the city its wealth. Lying on the Saale, which feeds the Elbe, it was also a river port. The composer George Frideric Handel was born here in 1685.

EASTERN TYROL, Austria (left)

The little church dedicated to St Korbinian sits on a hillock overlooking the Pustertal valley in Austria's eastern Tyrol. Its treasures include works by Michael Pacher, better known for the stunning high altar he completed in 1482 in the church at St Wolfgang (now a health resort) in Upper Austria. Along the Pustertal's broad valley runs the Drau, which eventually flows into the Danube. On its north side are the Defereggen mountains, where pretty villages bask on a "sun terrace."

COLOGNE, Germany (right)

Cologne Cathedral appears like a haunting spirit from a Gothic tale, out of place with the modern, post-Second World War city around it. This is what aerial bombing did; suddenly gone forever were so many monuments, so many tangible links with the past.

ZURICH, Switzerland

The spire of St Peter's Church, which has clock faces measuring some 29 feet (9 meters) in diameter, looks out across Zurich, Switzerland's largest city. The camera has distorted the curve in the Limmat River, which runs in to the city from Lake Zurich (off to the right of the picture), past the twin towers of the Grossmünster, to the seventeenth-century Rathaus jutting out into the river on the far bank (near the center of the picture). The Rathaus is still used by the town and canton parliaments.

THE ROAD OF THE CELLARS,
Austria (left)

"Kellergasse" is the Road of the Cellars, a row of small farmhouses each sitting on top of cavernous basements where the produce of the gently rolling hills around them is kept. The strips of land, colored according to their state of cultivation, are all planted with vines. The loamy ground absorbs the sun's rays to make this region in Lower Austria, some 25 miles (40 kilometers) northeast of Vienna, one of the country's main wine-producing centers.

ST STEPHEN'S CATHEDRAL,
Vienna, Austria (right)

The diamond-patterned glazed-tile roof of St Stephen's Cathedral in Vienna, rebuilt since the Second World War, is so steeply pitched that at first glance it seems to rise up like a pointed tower. When the 450-foot (137-meter) south tower, known as "Steffl," was put up it was considered too proud and lofty, and plans for a matching tower on the north side were cut short. But the lower tower provided a firmer base for "Pummerin" ("Boomer"), Austria's largest bell.

LEIPZIG, Germany

This is a legacy of the Third Reich, which looked to mythology to inspire nationalism. The Nibelungen-Ring in Leipzig is a 1930s housing estate constructed in "mystical" rings around Siegfried Square. The composer Richard Wagner was born in the city in 1813. Lying on the confluence of three rivers 90 miles (145 kilometers) southwest of Berlin, Leipzig has been known as "the secret capital of east Germany." Goethe, who set *Faust* in one of its taverns, called it "little Paris."

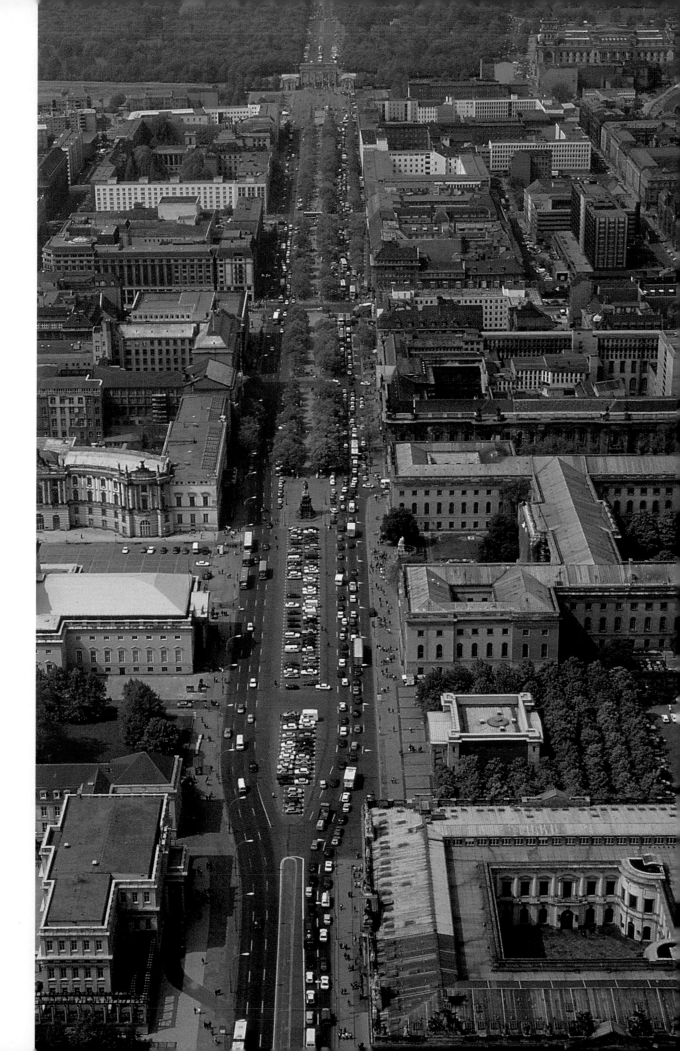

ENGLISH GARDEN,
Munich, Germany (left)

The Englischer Garten in Munich is
Europe's largest city park. On summer
evenings people bring picnics here to the
beer garden at the Chinese pagoda, where
they eat and drink at communal trestle
tables. The garden was designed in 1790
by the Anglo-American physician and
politician Lord Romford.

UNTER DEN LINDEN,
Berlin, Germany (right)

Unter den Linden (Under the Linden Trees)
is the best known street in Berlin. It was
laid out in the seventeenth century with
1000 linden trees and 1000 nut trees.
In the middle is a statue of Prussia's
Frederick the Great, born here in 1712.
At the far end lies the Brandenburg Gate,
once the symbol of a Germany divided
between East and West.

REINHARZ CASTLE, Germany

In the muted early morning light of a
German spring, trees not yet fully in leaf
are silhouetted in the pale waters of
a small lake belonging to Reinharz Castle.
Set among farmlands to the north of
Halle, this baroque "water castle" was
built in 1701.

NEUSCHWANSTEIN CASTLE,
Germany (left)

This is where Disneyland began. Neuschwanstein Castle was the greatest indulgence of the insane castle builder and Wagner patron, King Ludwig II of Bavaria. It was created by the theater designer Jank von Dollmann and built between 1886 and 1889. High on a rock, it overlooks the Allgäu mountains near the Austrian border. Each year 1.5 million people visit the castle, which was copied for the centerpiece of Disneyland in America.

SCHÖNBRUNN PALACE
Vienna, Austria (right)

Two grassy hearth rugs have been put down in the grand courtyard of Schönbrunn Palace in Vienna. This was the summer residence of the Habsburgs, bought in 1569. A century later it was remodeled and given a more modest aspect. Napoléon stayed here, and this is where Franz Joseph I (1830–1916) was born and died. In the palace grounds is the world's oldest zoo.

UPPER BAVARIA, Germany (left)

Snow wipes the color away from a winter scene in Upper Bavaria, south of Munich, reducing it to monochrome. This is Moosrain, part of the village of Gmund on the north shore of the Tegernsee. Holiday-makers come here year-round. In winter there are cross-country ski trails, while nearby mountains provide speedy slopes. In the summer it is hikers' terrain.

SAXONY, Germany (right)

In 1806 Napoléon made Saxony a kingdom. The region became part of the German Confederation and, later, the German Empire. After the First World War the monarchy was disolved and Saxony became a free state in the Weimar Republic. Located in East Germany, Saxony was abolished as a territory throughout the communist era. It was reinstated during the reunification of the East and West.

THE RHINE, Germany

Commercially, the Rhine is Europe's most important waterway. It flows from the Alps through Switzerland, along the Austrian, German and French borders, and through Germany and the Netherlands to the North Sea. In the Middle Rhine, between Mainz and Koblenz, is the fourteenth-century Pfalzgrafenstein (Customs House), still attending its island post.

MATTERHORN, Switzerland (left)

This snow-covered mountain is known as Mont Cervin in French and Monte Cervino in Italian. The famous Matterhorn stands 14 692 feet (4478 meters) in the Alps on the border between Switzerland and Italy. From the Swiss perspective the mountain looks like a solitary horn-shaped peak yet it is actually the end of a ridge.

REICHSTAG BUILDING, Berlin, Germany (right)

Designed by Paul Wallot, this Neo-Renaissance building was finished in 1894. Formerly the meeting place of the German national legislature, the Reichstag is one of Berlin's most recognizable buildings. It was used as a museum during the communist era. After the reunification the building was greatly renovated and restored. In 1990 the Bundestag, or Federal Assembly, of the reunified Germany first met in the Reichstag.

MAZURY, Poland

In Mazury, northeast Poland, a tractor systematically erases the color from a field. In this sparsely populated region is a sect of Russian Old Believers, a community that has lived here since the seventeenth century, intermarrying and keeping its archaic language alive.

Czechoslovakia became a state in 1918, created out of the fragmented Habsburg empire. Division between the predominantly urbanized Czechs and rural Slovaks led to their separation into the Czech and Slovak republics in 1993. Czech loyalties are centered on the magnificent and historic city of Prague, one of the most beautiful in all Europe and in itself an exhibition of European civilization.

A range of mountains dominates the Czech Republic and Slovakia, while Poland and Hungary are mostly flat, allowing the easy entry of armies. Here successive waves of invaders from the east have reached the limit

HEROES' SQUARE,
Budapest, Hungary

From here even the Angel Gabriel is looked down upon. His statue tops a pillar in the middle of Budapest's Heroes' Square: at its base are Prince Árpád and six other Magyar warrior chiefs who blazed a trail through the country in AD 896, 1000 years before this monument was constructed. Between the columns of the semicircular colonnade are statues of Hungary's rulers.

of their expansion—Mongols, Muslims, Soviet Communists—
and here, before the Second World War, lived the world's
greatest population of Jews, most of them murdered during
the Second World War by fellow-Europeans in the
concentration camps of Nazi-occupied Poland.

Coal is found in Poland and bauxite in Hungary, but
traditionally these have been agricultural lands with a labor
force of peasantry. Only in the west of the Czech Republic,
in old Bohemia and Moravia, is there an old, established
industrial base, and even now, when the whole area has
been homogenized by nearly half a century of communism,
the gilded cities of the old regimes contrast piquantly with
the poor villages of the countrysides. Yet these are states of
consequence, strong in their own loyalties, and forming a
kind of buffer, extending north and south across much of
Europe, between the venerable and elaborate cultures of the
west and Asia's even more ancient influence.

GDANSK, Poland

The individually styled gables of these colorful five-storey houses look
Dutch: some acutely angled, some stepped, and some with the
curvacious lines of a cello or violin. But they are not in Holland;
they are in Poland in the old town of Gdańsk, showing what links there
have been between northern Europe's neighbors for so many centuries.
Trade with Germany and Flanders via the Baltic was active in the ninth
century, and the prosperous building boom came in the
sixteenth and seventeenth centuries.

OLD WARSAW, Poland (left)

The whimsical tilt of the roofs and the simple house façades make this picture seem like the work of a naïve artist. This is Rynek Starego Miasta, the square at the heart of old Warsaw. It suffered in the systematic destruction of the city by the Nazis following the 1944 uprising, but immediately after the war it was reconstructed based on surviving photographs, engravings and paintings.

WARSAW, Poland (above)

Lined up in stoic silence, these housing blocks seem to be waiting for someone to tell them what to do. This is the Bródno quarter of Warsaw, a middle-class housing district that was built in the 1970s. Even though the buildings are spread out, the open areas between them are not large enough to prevent some buildings living in the shadows of others.

HLUBOKÁ CASTLE,
southern Bohemia,
Czech Republic

The British royal family may not recognize
it, but this is supposed to be a replica of
Windsor Castle. Hluboká Castle, founded in
the thirteenth century, was rebuilt in the
late nineteenth century. By the time it was
confiscated by the government in 1945 it
was the center of the largest private
domain in the then Czechoslovakia.
Situated in a park above the Vltava River,
it is open to the public.

PRAGUE, Czech Republic (left)

Prague 2, Vinohrady District was once the best address for officials and the upper middle class of the Czech Republic's capital. "Vinohrady" means vineyards, which is what this land just east of the old town was given over to until the last century. Ideally located, the garden squares were built to a modern urban design at the beginning of this century, but now pollution and deterioration in the buildings' fabric have forced its traditional residents further away.

CARLSBAD, Czech Republic (right)

This is where Europe's rich and royal used to come for their curative baths. Karlovy Vary in Bohemia, better known as Carlsbad, grew prosperous on its thermal springs after the main one was discovered in the fourteenth century. Charles IV was said to have been led to it by a deer while out hunting. The spa has twelve springs, which are still in use for cures and treatments, although the scaffolding on some of the buildings hints at the cost of maintaining the resort's rich architectural legacy.

MARIENBURG, Poland

Begun in 1274, the pink castle of
Marienburg was a major bastion of the
Teutonic Order of knights. Situated in
north Poland, just inland from Gdańsk,
it was a base for the knights' forays into
the east as they helped to carve out the
Baltic empire. In 1466 it came under
Polish administration, and today
medieval events are re-enacted there.

MAZURY, Poland (left)

Autumn colors the ancient woods of Mazury, northeast Poland, one of Europe's most bountiful natural regions. There are 90 nature reserves containing wild buffalo, Europe's largest elk herd, and the world's smallest forest ponies.

BUDAPEST, Hungary (right)

The settlements of Buda and Pest grew up on the banks of the Danube. Occupied by the Ottoman Turks for 150 years, it was really only after the revolution of 1848 against the Habsburgs that Budapest began to be transformed into a worthy European capital. Boulevards were laid out and grand buildings went up, among them the neo-Gothic Parliament House which stretches along the Pest bank of the river in the foreground of the picture. It was completed in 1904.

CHARLES BRIDGE,
Prague, Czech Republic

Charles Bridge is Prague's most delightful artery. Vehicles are no longer allowed on the 1980-foot (603-meter) bridge, which was designed in the fourteenth century by a 27-year-old architect, Peter Parler of Grund, who supposedly bonded its stones with mortar mixed with eggs. Its 30 statues were added in the eighteenth and nineteenth centuries. From the old town on the near bank of the Vltava, the bridge leads over the river to Malá Strana, the old noble quarter, and the city's castle.

SOUTHERN MORAVIA,
Czech Republic (left)

For mile upon mile the farmlands of southern Moravia are scratched clean and planted with fruit trees, in particular with apricots and peaches for which the region is famous. But the main crop comes from the vine, which thrives in the Czech Republic's sunniest corner. Summers are hotter and drier than in western Europe.

ST NICHOLAS'S CHURCH,
Prague, Czech Republic (right)

St Nicholas's in Old Town Square, Prague, wears a creamy white, well-starched gown beneath the worn green ruffs of its roof. There has been a church on this site since the thirteenth century, but its present form dates from 1732. In 1883, in a house just beside it, the writer Franz Kafka was born. The baroque age attracted artists and craftsmen to the city, patronized by the rich and noble foreigners who settled here.

ZWIERZYNIEC, Poland

The monastery of Bielany in Zwierzyniec
looks a remote refuge, but in fact it is just
a bus ride from Kraków. The monks belong
to the strict Cameldolite order, established
in 1604, which allows them no contact
with the outside world.

HVĚZDA SUMMER CASTLE,
Prague, Czech Republic (left)

Prague's Royal Game Reserve was founded
at Bilá Hora (White Mountain) by
Ferdinand I in 1534. Some 24 years later
his son, Archduke Ferdinand of Tyrol,
designed this three-story hunting lodge,
the Hvězda Summer Castle. Today it is
a museum for the works of writer Alois
Jirásek and painter Mikoláš Aleš.

MATTHIAS CHURCH,
Budapest, Hungary (right)

Hungarian kings did not rule by divine
right; they had to be elected, like
presidents. Matthias Corvinus was elected
in 1458 and ruled for 32 years, during
which time he founded a university and an
observatory, encouraged the arts, built up a
large library, and extended and decorated
this church in Budapest. St Matthias was
the coronation church of the Hungarian
kings. In the nineteenth century it was
substantially rebuilt and the colored roof
added. Inside is a treasure-house of history.

BUDAPEST, Hungary

Facing each other across the Danube are
Buda on the left and Pest on the right. The
two were not joined until 1839 when a
Scotsman, William Tierney Clark, designed
the Chain Bridge in the middle of the
picture. In 1872 the two towns, together
with Óbuda (old Buda), were merged into
the Hungarian capital of Budapest. The
grand Buda palace was built in the
nineteenth century.

THE EASTERNERS

ALBANIA ∾ BOSNIA AND HERZEGOVINA ∾ BULGARIA
CROATIA ∾ GREECE ∾ MACEDONIA ∾ ROMANIA
SLOVENIA ∾ TURKEY ∾ YUGOSLAVIA

In the southeast of Europe one feels the breath of Asia. Although it may be said that here, in classical Greece, European civilization was born, today the countries that lie between the Adriatic and the Black seas seem the least European parts of Europe. They also form the least homogenous part of the continent. Romania and Bulgaria make the difficult transition from communist states to capitalist democracies. Yugoslavia, for many years a multi-ethnic federation governed by its own brand of independent communism, has disintegrated. Yugoslavia today comprises only Serbia, Kosovo, Vojvodina and Montenegro. A bitter civil war led to Croatia, Slovenia, Macedonia and Bosnia-Herzegovina declaring independence in 1991.

Greece, where the idea of democracy was conceived, and Turkey, only a small portion of which lies within Europe at all, are democratic republics. Albania was the last of the hard-line Communist Peoples' Republic to switch to democracy in the early 1990s and is the poorest country of the continent.

But then none of these countries is naturally rich. Romania has oilfields which have been, during the twentieth century, one of Europe's chief strategic prizes. Yugoslavia has bauxite. Turkey has chrome. The vast majority of these peoples, however, have always lived by agriculture and pastoralism in terrain that is often harshly demanding. Sometimes

PÁTMOS ISLAND, Greece

For 300 years after the monastery of St John was built, no secular buildings were allowed on Pátmos, the smallest of Greece's Dodecanese islands, near the coast of Turkey. It was founded in 1088 and dedicated to the Apostle St John, who supposedly wrote The Apocalypse in a nearby cave while in exile. The monastery was the object of Byzantine emperors' devotions, and it became rich and well endowed.

it is hard to realize that one is in Europe at all, so remote do these hard flinty places feel from the lush meadows and grand mountain landscapes of the west. The Turkish metropolis of Istanbul (formerly Constantinople and Byzantium) is indeed almost an epitome of Asianism, crowned as it is by minarets and clamoring with bazaars directly upon the Bosporus. And on the island of Crete, the greatest of Greece's innumerable offshore islands, there are times when the sky is darkened by dust-clouds blowing across the sea from Libya.

Spiritually, too, these countries are instinct with the exotic. The legends of classical Greece speak of an ancient world that looked to the east for its sources of inspiration and delight. The glorious Byzantine buildings that ornament the region remember a time when the epicenter of Europe was on the edge of Asia. The cities are often reminiscent of Levantine cities, pungent with spice. The Orthodox Christianity that prevails in these parts is a scented, mystical, hauntingly lyrical version of the creed, and the local histories are full of eastern intruders— Persians, Mongols, Russians, Turks.

Turks especially, because for several centuries almost all these territories formed part of the Ottoman Empire. The Turkish armies were turned back at the gates of Vienna in 1529, but it was not until the twentieth century that they were obliged to withdraw from the last of their European conquests. For much of their modern history then, these countries lived under Islam. Greece itself, that lodestar of democrats everywhere, was the first to throw off the thrall and thus rekindle among the Europeans a passion for national liberty that has been intermittently blazing ever since.

ALEXANDER NEVSKI MEMORIAL CHURCH, Sofia, Bulgaria

Five hundred years of Turkish occupation did not extinguish Sofia's Christian faith.
In 1878 Bulgaria was "liberated" from the Turks by the Russians, and in gratitude this
gold-topped church was built. The Alexander Nevski Memorial Church at the heart of the
country's capital is named after a thirteenth-century prince who was patron saint
of Alexander II, Tsar of Russia at the time of the liberation.

Yet Islam, and the Asia that conceived it, has never quite withdrawn from these regions of Europe. In some parts it remains a living religion. Approximately 13 percent of the population of Bulgaria are practising Muslims; in Bosnia and Herzegovina and Kosovo whole towns and villages are still predominantly Muslim; Istanbul is a half-Islamic city; and in Albania Islam was the almost universal religion until, in 1967, all religion was officially abolished. In many other regions, even in Greece itself, it remains an elusive echo, expressed in old buildings, in attitudes and values, in the way a woman wears her shawl or a man strikes a deal. Asia is present in Europe still, in these chequered countries of the continental east.

SAVA RIVER VALLEY, Slovenia

The crops seem well combed around this isolated church and graveyard in the Sava River valley in Slovenia. The river rises near here in the Karavanke mountains, which resemble the neighboring Austrian Alps, and flows southeast to meet the Danube at Belgrade. The region is popular for walking and skiing.

ISTANBUL, Turkey

From out of the blue on the far side of the Bosporus comes the continent of Asia: Europe is at an end. In human terms, the border is not so straightforward. Istanbul, formerly Byzantium and Constantinople, was capital of a Christian empire from AD 328 until 1453, when it became the Muslim Ottomans' power base. It is the only city in the world to straddle two continents; less than 10 percent of Turkey is in Europe. Built on seven hills crowned with architectural splendors, the old city rises above the Golden Horn. The Suleimanye is the finest of four mosques built by the greatest of the sultans, Suleiman the Magnificent, who ruled from 1520 to 1556 and brought all Asia Minor, the Middle East and part of North Africa under Ottoman control.

OUR LADY OF THE ROCKS,
Bay of Kotor, Yugoslavia

Built in the sixteenth century, this church
stands on an artificial island in the Bay of
Kotor. Sailors heaped stones and boulders
onto a reef here until it was solid enough
to sustain the building of the church.

DURMITOR MOUNTAINS,
Yugoslavia (left)

Huddled like a family of sleeping prehistoric animals, the Durmitor mountains in the heart of Montenegro are the most dramatic in Yugoslavia. Rising to 8270 feet (2520 meters) they are the harsh homeland of a rugged people who have never been subjugated. A national park now includes rich meadows, forests and lakes, as well as mountain peaks.

BUCHAREST, Romania (right)

Rolled out like a patterned carpet for the city's dignitaries, Union Boulevard in Bucharest leads to Romania's parliament building. To create this tree-lined street of apartment blocks and new shops, many historic buildings were torn down.

PLOIEŞTI, Romania (left)

These are the shapes of twentieth-century industry: spheres and cylinders, sheds and smokestacks, pipes and drums. The Brazi petrochemical plant near the oil fields of Ploieşti north of Bucharest covers 1235 acres (500 hectares) and processes a quarter of the country's crude oil. Set up in 1934, it was greatly expanded in the 1960s. The 50 specialized units convert crude oil into more than 100 different products, including refined petrol, carbolic acid and raw material for the plastics industry.

GRATARUL, Romania (above)

Who will make the effort to go to Gratarul church this Sunday to pray? It is not, in fact, miles from anywhere, but just 5 miles (8 kilometers) outside the small city of Călăraşi, southeast Romania. This region of the Danube floodplains just east of Bucharest is very fertile. There are few walls or windbreaking trees to stop the late-summer harvesting machines from threshing from one horizon to the other. Only the church might get in the way.

MYKONOS, Greece

No matter how many tourists go to the
Greek island of Mykonos every year,
they cannot spoil its glaring loveliness.
Nothing can dim the dazzling white cubes
of its houses standing over the darkest
of seas. There are several privately owned
Orthodox chapels, like the one in the left
of the picture.

CORINTH CANAL, Greece (left)

Ancient Greeks wanting to sail from the Gulf of Corinth to the Saronic Gulf would sometimes drag their boats across the 4-mile (6-kilometer) isthmus between mainland Greece and the Peloponnese. It wasn't until 1893 that a canal was properly dug to shorten the trip. For sailors it is a claustrophobic experience: the walls rise vertically on each side, and it is barely wider than a ship's beam.

MONTENEGRO, Yugoslavia (right)

This is the heart of Montenegro, Yugoslavia's mountainous southwest, which in 1910 became a kingdom under Nikola I, who dispensed the law beneath a tree. He was known as the "Bismarck of the Balkans" and 15 foreign embassies were established in the kingdom's capital, Cetinje. These are the hills that surround the plateau on which Cetinje was built. It lies 2070 feet (630 meters) above the Bay of Kotor on the Adriatic, 9 tortuous miles (15 kilometers) away. Only 16 000 people now live in the historic town.

THE PARTHENON, Athens, Greece

Democracy, philosophy, drama ... all
the essentials of western civilization
crystalized around this green limestone
table. At its summit is the Parthenon. Built
between 447 and 432 BC by Pericles,
it contained a large gold and ivory statue
of the city's protectress, Athena. The
Parthenon was lavishly decorated with
friezes and sculptures carved in marble by
the famous sculptor, Pheidias.

RILA, Bulgaria (left)

High up in the Rila mountains near the border with Greece, Ivan of Rila founded this monastery in the tenth century, and it was reconstructed some 400 years later. Today the monks' cells are guestrooms, and most of the complex is a museum. Its treasures of artworks and icons, as well as 16 000 manuscripts and books printed on the premises, were accumulated beyond the gaze of the occupying Turks.

BELOGRADCHIK, Bulgaria (right)

The twisting mounds and stacks of weathered sandstone around Belogradchik can appear to take on human or animal forms. In the extreme northwest corner of Bulgaria just below the Danube, they marked the Roman empire's northern boundary. They provided natural strongholds that the Romans and Turks were quick to exploit: the fort of Kaleto is at the foot of the hills in this picture. Nearby are the extensive caves of Magura, where paintings in bat guano were made in the early Bronze Age.

SANTORÍNI, Greece

The volcanic island of Santorini (also called Thera) in the southern Cyclades is famed for its spectacular cliff wall that rises out of the sea. From here the land's altitudes are not evident. Instead there is a pattern of fields and the tendrils of thin roads leading from the white flare of Oía.

INDEX

ACKNOWLEDGMENTS

Weldon Owen wish to thank the following people for their help with this project: Peta Gorman, Puddingburn Publishing Services (index), Nick Szentkuti.

Photography
Torbjörn Andersson, Yann Arthus-Bertrand, Max Dereta, Georg Gerster, Leo Meier, Oddbjørn Monsen, Horst Munzig, Daniel Philippe, Georg Riha, Guido Alberto Rossi, Michael St Maur Sheil, Emil Schulthess, Thomas Stephan, Adam Woolfitt.
All photography is copyright Weldon Owen Inc. except: 4–5, 21, 24–25, 41, 62–63, 74–75, 82–83, 85, 105, 106–107, 114–115, 116, 120, 121, 122–123, 157, 166–167, 197, 201, 246, front cover Corbis; 124 Jason Hawkes; 27, 30–31, 94–95, 110–111, 200, Tony Stone.

Maps
Ian Faulkner, Laurie Whiddon